Young, Divorced and Fabulous

Four Women Share their Journeys, their Friendship and their Sisterly Advice on Embracing Second Chances

*Karen Jerabek, Michelle Joyce,
Michelle Nicolet & Michelle Denicola Poole*

Authors' Note: Our memoirs were written based on our memories of conversations and events that happened during our marriages and divorces. Some names and identifying details have been changed to protect the privacy of individuals. Parts of this book were previously published under the title, The Mini Marriage: 5 Bite Sized Memoirs of Young Divorce, which is no longer in publication.

Book cover design and illustration by Damonza

First edition, 2014

Printed in the United States of America

ISBN-10: 1494277921
ISBN-13: 978-1494277925

www.YoungDivorcedandFabulous.com

for our amazing friends and families,

*Thank you for always believing in us
and for all of the love and support
you have given to us throughout the years.*

Contents

I'm Getting Divorced!
Now, what the hell am I going to do?

Divorce sucks. There, I said it. S-U-C-K-S sucks. You're left feeling like you're going to die. Yet, that doesn't happen. And, then you find yourself sitting in a slumped pile on the floor with tear stained cheeks, wondering what the hell am I going to do?!!

Seriously, what the hell am I going to do?

At 27 years old, I thought my life had been neatly packaged into the happily ever after variety when it all came crashing down around me on my second anniversary. I found myself staring at the door marked divorce. As I hesitantly reached for the door knob, I knew as I stepped over the

1

threshold, that I was, for better or worse, starting my journey toward answering that nagging, foreboding question - What the hell am I going to do?

After endless Google searches, I found myself down the street at my local Barnes & Noble bookstore, still searching for answers. I stood motionless in front of the shelves as my eyes scanned the book titles. One by one, I picked them up, leafed through the pages and placed them back on the shelf. Nothing. I turned to the shelves behind me, repeating this same process. Pick a book, leaf through the pages, put it back.

Confused, I looked around to make sure I was in the right place. *Self-Help, Relationships, Divorce.* Yep, right place, but where were the books I needed? There were plenty of divorce books, but nothing seemed to fit my situation. I didn't have children. There were hardly any assets to speak of and I certainly didn't expect any alimony. I wasn't going through a midlife divorce. Hell, I wasn't even 30, but I was still getting divorced and I still needed to know how to deal with it.

I was about to give up when my eyes landed on *The Starter Marriage* by Pamela Paul. Ugh. Is that what this is called, a starter marriage? I rolled my eyes to avoid the tears from dripping down my face. I don't want people accusing me of going into my marriage with the intention of just trading up if it doesn't work. I picked up the book with a sigh, hoping that I'd connect with something inside its pages.

Pamela Paul, who had also gone through her own self-described starter marriage, wrote an analytical take on marriage and divorce under the age of 35 examining the statistics and perceptions of young divorce. After flipping through her book, I was disappointed that I didn't find stories about people like me in the pages. There were interviews with young divorced people, but it seemed like they were still confused about why their marriages ended and were spouting common media explanations. I wasn't immature, lazy or lacking commitment. I had tried hard to make my marriage work. I didn't consider it a test marriage until I got a better one. My marriage was real and was meant to last forever. Unfortunately life didn't turn out that way and I ended up with a short marriage, *not* a starter marriage. While the statistics were interesting, what I was craving was a sense that I wasn't alone...that there were people out there just like me. Disappointed, I put the book back on the shelf, realizing that the support I was seeking wasn't going to be found in those pages.

Back to square one, I thought, as I settled in front of my computer that night. The blue screen kept me company on nights like this; nights when I couldn't sleep and felt like I was the only one going through a young divorce. I clicked on page after page looking for some kind of support. One last time, I thought and then I'm giving up. I said a small prayer that I could find someone, somewhere who would understand what I was going through. Click. A hesitant smile spread across my face, not quite believing what I was looking at - a message board specifically for young women going through a divorce. I excitedly clicked on the link and started reading post after post. Jackpot!

Tears streamed down my face as I was introduced to women who were my age and who were going through a divorce without children. *There really are people out there that are just like me.* I quickly typed a brief message, trying to sum up my story in a paragraph or two. Sobbing as I typed, I was overwhelmed by the emotions that I kept bottled up for so long. I found myself admitting to these strangers that even though I've been married for only a brief time, it's over and it looks like I'm getting divorced. I don't want to be divorced. I never wanted to be divorced. I planned on being married forever. And yet, here I am, alone in the house that was supposed to be filled with our dreams. Instead, it's where they're suffocating and dying. There will be no more anniversaries. There will be no babies. There will be no future. Admitting this, even to these online strangers, was more painful than I expected. I choked on my tears, wiped my face with my sleeve and hit submit. Then I collapsed and sobbed until my eyes couldn't produce any more tears. My only hope was that I would pass out from exhaustion and sleep would give me a temporary reprieve from feeling completely devastated.

In the morning, I logged back onto the message board and there were already several welcome messages. I cried some more as I read the words of encouragement, understanding and sympathy that these women, who didn't even know me, were offering. I felt like I had finally been offered a lifeline. It was like I had been drowning and now I had found my safety raft. I was not alone. Thank God, I'm not alone!

Several of the women I met through that message board have remained my dear friends. I spent lonely night after lonely night at my computer typing to these women I barely knew, sharing the anguishing details of my marriage and my impending divorce while purging the anger and sadness that consumed me. It was a relief to know that we were all going through the heartache, the loneliness and the despair that comes with having a marriage fall apart. We were there for each other through the darkest days of our divorces and we forged such a deep friendship with each other that we consider ourselves sisters...*divorce sisters*. And, we're here to bring that sisterhood to you.

In the following pages, you'll meet the original divorce sisters, Michelle Joyce, Michelle Nicolet, Michelle Denicola Poole and me, Karen Jerabek. We're four women from different parts of the country, different backgrounds, different lifestyles, who got married when we were in our 20s and divorced before we reached 30. We never thought that we would be among the "divorced", but here we are. Each of us fell in love with men that we thought we'd spend our lives with, share our hopes and dreams of the future with, have children with and grow old with. We entered our marriages thinking that they would be strong, successful marriages. None of us considered the possibility that it might not work out. None of us considered the possibility of divorce. It wasn't something that crossed our minds. We were in love and we were going to make our marriages work. *Other people get divorced, not us.* Within a couple of years, all of our marriages were over and we became those "other people." We became "divorcees."

None of us had just one fight and walked out the door like it's often portrayed in the media. We tried and tried and tried some more to make our marriages work. But, they didn't work and we refused to resign ourselves to unhappy, unfulfilling marriages. It wasn't until we felt we had exhausted all resources and all means to save our marriages that we finally accepted divorce.

Even though there are very few resources for women like us, we're part of a social phenomenon sweeping the country. Young divorces are commonly portrayed as merely

6

an inconvenience for the couple and not the life altering and traumatic events that they really are. Despite the short term nature of these unions, they are entered into with the hope that they'll last a lifetime. When they end, couples typically experience an intense grief over the loss of their marriage which is rarely acknowledged in our society.

Since we didn't have children many people shrugged off our divorces as being easy. It's assumed that you can simply slide right back into your single lifestyle like you didn't miss a beat. And it's true, there are no outward signs that you've just emerged from a divorce. But, on the inside, you're not the same person you were before you were married. What we discovered is that almost everyone struggles to find themselves as they go through a divorce.

Short, young marriages aren't just a Hollywood trend either. Not only did Katy Perry, Olivia Wilde, Jessica Simpson, Avril Lavigne, Jennifer Aniston, Jennifer Lopez, Kim and Khloe Kardashian get divorced after brief marriages, so did your neighbor and your co-worker and you probably didn't even realize it. Everyone knows that the divorce rate in the United States is about 50%, but what we didn't realize was how many of these divorces were from short marriages until we started researching the US Census Bureau's statistics. Marriage is most susceptible to divorce during the first few years with the average length of marriage being eight years.

The average age for people going through their first divorce is 30. Almost 2.5 million divorces happen each year in the United States. Not only did we realize that there were a handful of other women just like us out there, but there were literally millions of them. After seeing how each of us struggled to find support and hope despite how common young divorce really is, we decided to write this book to reach out to women everywhere who are young and divorcing.

When friends and family don't understand what you're going through, it can be an isolating, depressing and lonely feeling. The only people who really understood our heartache and devastation, was each other. Divorce is a painful experience no matter your age or the length of your marriage or whether you had children. The next four chapters are memoirs from each of us about our marriages and our divorces. We share with you our stories of anguish, confusion and eventually triumph over our divorces. In chapter six, we offer a dose of sisterly advice on how to move on with your life and we answer that nagging question, what the hell am I going to do now? We also share updates on where our lives have gone in the years since our divorces as we embraced our second chances. There is a light at the end of the tunnel. The four of us have made it through that harrowing experience of divorce and we're now shining that light for you to join us.

If you're going through a divorce, feeling completely alone and wondering, "What the hell am I going to do?" This book is your answer.

You are not alone.

We understand what you're going through.

We get it.

And we're here for you!

When you're done reading this book, you'll be inspired, just like we were, to answer that question by proudly standing up and saying, *I'm going to be Young, Divorced and Fabulous – that's what!*

We welcome you with open arms to the divorce sisterhood!

Pulled into the Closet

By: Karen Jerabek

Pulling into an empty spot in the garage, I put my car in park and turn off the engine. Checking my watch, checking my paperwork, I take a deep breath. Closing my eyes, I take another deep breath. I really wish this breathing stuff would work. With a sigh, I turn off my cell phone and get out of the car. Ready or not, my life is about to change.

The metal detectors greet me as soon as I enter the courthouse. Glancing around at the other people in the building, I notice that not a single person looks happy to be here. I don't blame them. Who would be happy to spend their morning in the courthouse? Standing amidst the sea of

11

grim expressions, we wait for the elevator. One of the three elevator doors open and most of the people in the hallway cram in. I stand back, opting to wait for the next one. A man standing to my right offers me a feeble smile, indicating that he's going to wait as well.

We walk into the second elevator that's headed up. After several stops and people filtering on and off, we both step out on the ninth floor. Nervously glancing around, we both decide to head to the left. I ask him which courtroom he is looking for and he indicates the same one that I'm headed to, the courtroom that handles the divorce proceedings. At least I know I'm not the only one going through this today.

The roster with my name on it is posted to the courtroom door. I don't allow myself to hesitate. I enter the courtroom with as much self confidence and determination as I can muster. This will be a simple proceeding and it will be over relatively quickly, I remind myself. The room is half filled and it's very quiet. Walking to the end of the first long, narrow bench, I sit down and let out a long breath. "Would you mind if I sat next to you?" asks the man I met in the elevator. "Oh, no. Not at all," I smile as he sits down next to me, waiting for the judge to arrive.

As we check our paperwork for the millionth time, we discuss our nerves and the proceedings that will come and offer brief backgrounds on our marriages and our divorces. I

12

feel completely dazed, but there is such a sense of relief to have someone to talk to – a divorce buddy. I keep wiping my sweaty hands on my pants. They're the gray pants that go with my "interviewing" suit. I'm wearing a simple black sweater with it and black heels, looking somber and respectful, almost like I'm going to a funeral. Indeed, that's how I feel. My marriage languished for a long time, unable to have new life breathed into it. And, now it's time for it to be laid to rest. Shifting my legs on the bench I hope that I won't sweat so much that my pants stick to my legs when it's time to get up. Looking around, I note the pained expressions of the people who will be officially ending their marriages today. The courtroom is now full and people are standing against the wall. It shouldn't surprise me to see so many people given the current divorce statistics, but somehow it does.

The bailiff enters the room and I know that the time has come. He explains the proceedings and asks us to get our paperwork out and write the date on each of the forms. It's exactly four years to the day of my first date with my husband. Well, he's my soon to be ex-husband, my former husband, my first husband…whatever you want to call him. I haven't decided which way I'll describe him yet. All I know is that in less than an hour, he will no longer, legally, be my husband.

When I met him over four years ago, I was drawn to him immediately. I can't quite explain it. It was magnetic and almost felt out of my control. A couple months later, after developing a casual friendship, we had our first date. We took my dog, Bailey, to the park and spent the afternoon together outside. I fell hard and fast for him. He was thoughtful, caring, protective and simply wonderful. Being with him made me happy and I felt so alive, and for the first time, I felt completely safe. It was impossible to stop smiling.

A few days later, he came over to take me out on another date. It was spring and my allergies were in overdrive. I was congested, my eyes were red and swollen, and I was miserable. We started our date by running to Target to get some medicine. The back of the box said adults could take one or two tablets. Since my allergies were really bothering me and I wanted to enjoy my date, I popped two in my mouth and swallowed them with some water. Bad move. Usually I feel a little sleepy when I take one pill. Two pills made me practically comatose. Struggling just to keep my eyes open, I lay on the sofa with my head in his lap. "I'm sorry that I'm such a lousy date. You can leave if you want," I offered. He looked down at me as he tucked a strand of my hair behind my ear, "There isn't any other place that I'd rather be." I fell in love with him in that instant, not because he said those words, but because he really meant them. He was really there for me in a way other men had not been. He stroked my hair and sang along to the radio as I drifted in and out that night.

After a whirlwind courtship, we were married on a beach in the Bahamas seven months later. We were giddy through the entire ceremony. My favorite line of our vows was, "With this ring, I give you my heart. I have no greater gift to give." On that day, we each gave our heart completely to the other, or so I thought. It seemed like such a perfect day.

Inevitably, the honeymoon had to end. We had to leave the resort, the beach, and the frozen drinks behind. Feeling rested and happy, we boarded the plane back home with our new tans and our new rings. I thought that we would be heading into the blissful newlywed phase filled with romance and hot sex. Instead, it was back to the daily grind with jobs, bills, dogs, and all that tediously boring stuff that makes your life exceedingly stressful. There was no romance and definitely no hot sex.

We began our marriage trying to meld our lifestyles together, but it was more like a train wreck than the joyful cohesion of two lives. Within the first week, we were flying to a funeral. The very next weekend we decided to get a second dog. She was an exuberant, demonic puppy that destroyed the sofa, the carpet and refused to sleep at night. Then Thanksgiving and Christmas arrived and decisions about

15

traveling and in-laws had to be made. The pressure to reproduce was also mounting by my in-laws. I felt exhausted and stressed. We were arguing a lot and I began to wonder, what kind of marriage did I get myself into? I knew that half of all marriages end in divorce, but I never thought that I would be included in that statistic. Now, I wasn't so sure.

This startling realization made me examine my marriage. I had thought that being in love was all that was needed to create a strong, happy union. Despite our love and being best friends, we were having a hard time living together as husband and wife. We argued over how much time we should spend together, what activities we should do together, how we should budget our money and the list went on and on. It was obvious that we lacked compatibility.

I found myself married to a man I didn't even know. He wasn't the man I fell in love with. That man had vanished and I wondered if he ever truly existed at all. Gone were the days of walking the dogs together. Gone were the weekend shopping trips. Gone were the evenings spent laughing in restaurants. Gone were the late nights spent talking. Gone were the smiles from both of our faces. While we were dating, he gave me everything I wanted, but after we were married he said that he had done those things to make me happy, not because they were what he truly wanted to do. I thought we loved the same things but in fact, we had almost nothing in common.

A depression started to creep in and I started to sleep all the time, not having any of the energy that I used to have. The world felt like it was caving in on me. He spent every night getting virtually no sleep because the puppy was ready to play after sleeping all day while we worked. He became resentful of this situation, but I couldn't seem to snap out of it. I had never been depressed and it took me several months to realize that a change in birth control pills was probably a contributing factor or that's at least what I told myself. I went off the pill and let my body stabilize for a couple months. Some of my perkiness came back, but I certainly wasn't the happy, bouncy person I was the year before. Another contributing factor to my depression and probably the main one was my shock and disappointment that I didn't have the marriage I expected. Not knowing how to deal with that let down made life feel very hard.

Searching for external reasons for our unhappiness, I refused to consider any internal ones. We had spent the past several months paying an enormous fee to rent month to month in our 630 square foot apartment. We had talked about moving, but didn't want to be tied into a lease because he wanted to look for a job since he was miserable in the one he had. We agreed to move wherever he got a job offer. A new

17

city and a new life was what I dreamed of, a place where we could have the marriage I had envisioned. My frustration mounted as he did virtually no job searching so I decided to tackle the feat myself. All we needed was for one of us to get a job and then the other could find work after we moved. I updated my resume and started submitting it. When I started to get some interest, he had negative comments (some accurate and some not) about each position and I finally gave up looking.

Since it was becoming obvious that we weren't moving out of state any time soon, I decided that we needed to move into a bigger place. That was sure to make us happier. Living in a tiny apartment with two dogs was more than cramped. Having more space, would definitely relieve the stress I thought so we found a cute house to rent. It was twice the size of the apartment and had three bedrooms and it was also two blocks from a small, private lake with a paved walking trail. The landlord seemed nice and sounded like he'd be flexible if we needed to adjust our lease. I still had hopes of moving out of the city; they were just not immediate anymore.

After we moved in, he decided that he didn't want any responsibility for either of our dogs. If I wanted to keep them both, then I had to handle all aspects of taking care of them. When we got our puppy right after we were married, I pictured us walking the dogs together; one for each of us.

Going on outdoor adventures was my ideal way to spend the day and finding a husband who shared that same outlook had been important to me. When we dated, we did those sorts of things all the time. But, now that we were married, nothing was how I thought it would be.

Handling two dogs on two leashes by myself was challenging as I took on the full responsibility of their care. It wasn't easy and there were several times I almost got my arm pulled out of socket or got wrapped around a tree. In time, I got used to it and the dogs and I settled into a routine. I hoped that once he had rested up from the sleepless puppy nights he had endured that he'd want to go for walks with us again. That day never came.

He began withdrawing and started spending more and more time alone. His shopping habits were getting more and more out of hand, also. We couldn't afford all of the cds that he bought. He seemed unconcerned about debt. Never carrying a balance on my credit card, I freaked out when we suddenly had unnecessary bills that we couldn't pay off at the end of the month. We had agreed before we got married that credit cards would be for emergencies only and that we'd budget our money so that each of us could have some spending cash. When I would remind him of this agreement, he'd become angry. He didn't like feeling lectured. He was seven years older than me and said that he didn't need to be told how to do things.

I was afraid that our different outlooks on money could possibly lead us to a divorce. Not wanting to get divorced, I stopped opening the bills. The anxiety was overwhelming every time I'd see a credit card balance and I almost had panic attacks trying to figure out how to pay off our bills. I couldn't enjoy anything, not even buying a magazine, because I saw it as money that wasn't going toward our bills. This was the main argument we had over and over and over again until I finally opted out. I told him that he could handle all the financial decisions and just keep me up to date on the checkbook balance so that I could buy groceries. Not wanting to fight and not wanting to get divorced, I decided to trust that he'd take care of me just like he was asking me to do. When I gave up control, we stopped fighting and things were relatively calm again, but it was evident that there was still something missing.

Looking for yet another external cause for our unhappiness, I decided that I was too stressed out with an unreasonable work load, establishing a new marriage and all the responsibilities of the dogs. I suggested that I quit my job so I could fully focus on our marriage, thinking that if I could just invest more time and more energy, my marriage would become what I had dreamed it would be. Taking two months off during the summer and then looking for another job seemed like it would be the best thing for us. We could manage the bills on his salary, but we'd have to be careful with our spending. I'd get paid out for my unused vacation and he was up for a salary increase, so that would offset the loss of my income for a couple months. He agreed with my suggestion and I turned in my resignation.

Leaving my job was sad for me even though it had its stressful moments. I liked what I did, but now I was married. My husband and my marriage were my top priority. I was willing to do whatever I could to make my marriage better, so I devoted myself to domestication even though it terrified me to give up my financial independence. Taking on all the cooking and cleaning responsibilities and doing everything for the dogs would take stress off of him. He'd be able to relax more and we could start enjoying our marriage, I reasoned. If I could be June Cleaver, I was confident that I'd finally have a happy husband.

After quitting my job, I also started writing. Reading and writing were two things that I always loved to do when I was growing up. In high school, I wrote a lot of poetry and some short stories but stopped during college when I realized that so many other college students were doing the same thing. My self confidence fizzled as I realized I wasn't "special." Fearing that I had no talent, I gave up writing

21

altogether. One day, I shared my passion for writing with my husband and he encouraged me to let go of my insecurity and go back to it without worrying about it being perfect. He told me that I should do it because I loved it and because I had something to say, something to share. When he read what I wrote, he could be somewhat critical but the initial encouragement from him was the best thing that I got out of our marriage. It reignited that spark, that passion for me. When I wasn't trying to be June Cleaver, I was engrossed in my writing.

That summer rejuvenated me. The dogs had settled down somewhat, I wasn't so stressed out and I was happy that I had the time to focus on taking care of my husband. I cherished the simple memories we created together like grilling out, dancing in the living room and going to a couple of movies together. We stayed home most of the time because he didn't like going out, but we seemed to have fun spending time together again. It certainly felt like the tide was beginning to turn. Our marriage seemed to be improving and I felt hopeful that we were on the right track.

We had also been talking about taking a trip together at the end of the summer. It was going to be our first married vacation. I didn't really care where we were going, just that we were going someplace new together. Engrossing myself in research, I planned it all out, finding the cheapest plane tickets and a great hotel. But, when it came time to book the trip, he said that we really didn't have the money to go. Saddened, I offered to research a cheaper place for us to stay, but he said that we couldn't go. I didn't understand how we didn't have money to go when he was coming home with bags of stuff all the time. But, that was precisely the reason. He was spending a lot of money and was putting a lot of charges on the credit cards. Feeling extremely disappointed, my only solace was that we weren't going to add the expense of a trip to the credit cards too. He told me that he had the credit cards under control and that I needed to trust him and that he wasn't going to be buying any extra stuff anymore. Agreeing with him, I tried to keep my anxiety about our bills to myself and trust that we'd be okay in the end. I worried that we wouldn't be, but I didn't know what else to do.

The end of the summer arrived and I knew I needed to start looking for a job. Talk of moving had surfaced again. Not wanting to get a new job for only a couple months, I offered to continue staying home and spend my days job searching and researching positions for him. Our marriage seemed more solid and I thought that he'd be ready to move now. After countless hours of research, none of the positions seemed to be what he wanted and he didn't apply to one of them. The economy had also declined and there weren't as many possibilities. He suggested that we hold off on moving until the economy improved. His job was pretty secure and it seemed like the best choice was to stay put.

While we were going back and forth on the decision to move, I continued to write. Getting up early with the dogs, I'd make his lunch and send him off to work with a kiss. Then the dogs and I would go for a walk and I'd spend the morning typing away at the computer. A home cooked meal greeted him each night when he came home. I didn't open a single bill that summer because not knowing kept me calm and reduced the turbulence in our relationship. Ignorance was safer, I reasoned. Staying home and taking care of my husband made me happy. Once we figured out where we were going to live, I thought that maybe it would be time to start our family.

We celebrated our first anniversary that fall. It had been a rough year with a lot of changes and a lot of chaos. I thought that since we'd survived it together, that we could make it through anything. We had struggled and, yet, we were still standing. Our love and our dedication had won out and we seemed to finally be settling into a comfortable rhythm with each other. As we toasted our marriage, it felt like a battle victory.

During a job search, I found an educational contract position that I could do from home on a contract basis which was perfect and I continued to look for a full time opportunity. He didn't feel like I could handle all of the responsibilities with the dogs and working full time and he told me that he wouldn't help out at home. He thought if I tried to do it all, I'd go back to being overly stressed out again. I thought I could handle it, but he didn't want to try. He said that I had to get rid of the dogs if I really wanted to work full time. My dogs are my family so getting rid of them wasn't an option in my mind so I stopped looking for a full time job and did the contract work when it was available.

Our second year of marriage was very lonely for me. Even though we almost never had a fight, got along great and were best friends, we lived like roommates instead of husband and wife. We never went anywhere or did anything together. He liked to unwind on his own on the weekends and went off by himself while I stayed home with the dogs. After work, he'd frequently take a nap or listen to music until dinner was ready. We'd spend about an hour eating together and talking. After dinner, he'd get on the computer or listen to more music alone. We watched TV shows and movies together once in a while but not frequently. Life was very mundane. I would suggest new things for us to do; he was uninterested in any of it. He didn't want to go on vacation. He didn't want to go to the movies. He didn't want to go out to dinner. He didn't want to go hiking. Once in a while I could convince him to take me with him when he went cd or book shopping, but that was it.

He seemed increasingly overwhelmed by being married. I started going to visit my parents more often so that I could give him some solitude on the weekends. If I could just give him his space, I trusted that he'd give me more time and attention when he was able to. Not asking for anything, I tried to just let everything be. Sadness and loneliness encompassed me but I didn't know what else to do. As I focused on his needs, I neglected my own. If I endured the current state of our marriage for a little while longer, I believed things would get better. I lived for the day when life would become what I had hoped it would be.

Family and friends kept saying that we needed to get out more and do more things together. They didn't understand why we hardly spent any time together and, honestly, I didn't understand it either. All I knew was that he couldn't or wouldn't give me more. I loved him and I was committed to my marriage and would do anything to make it work. And so, I gave him space hoping that he'd become more comfortable with our marriage; the marriage we had agreed to create together before taking our vows.

I dreamed of the life I wanted and I hoped that we could find a way to create that together. I wanted him to be relaxed and happy. I wanted to take trips together. I wanted to go to the park with the dogs. I wanted to go out for a fun date night once in a while. I wanted a family. In essence, I wanted the American Dream. Holding onto that dream was the only thing that kept me going every day.

Perhaps a romantic vacation would be just what we needed to reunite us, I hoped. We'd be able to leave all the daily stresses behind us and focus on each other for an entire week. I was convinced that we'd come home more in love than ever. The disappointment of him canceling our trip during our first year of marriage still stung but here was our second chance. Some more contract work had been lined up for me so I excitedly told him that I wanted to save all the money I was making and put it towards a trip to Paris. What could be more wonderful and romantic than a week in Paris? Researching it was fun for me as I found the best deals and created a list of places for us to go, envisioning walking hand in hand next to the Seine River. When the prices started to creep up, I told him that it was time to book. He said that he had hoped we'd be able to go but it just wasn't going to work out. The credit card bills had grown significantly and a trip would be too much for us to do. I was devastated. He obviously wasn't taking care of our finances like he promised. He let me spend tons of time planning and dreaming about this vacation only to decide against it at the last minute. I was embarrassed because my family and friends knew I'd been planning this trip and how excited I was about it. Trying to salvage our vacation plans, I suggested a smaller one or even a weekend getaway together, but he turned down those ideas also. All the money I'd saved for Paris went on his credit card. He still didn't want me to get a full time job, but I found a part time job instead. The extra income could go on the credit cards too.

On our second anniversary, he came home agitated and extremely stressed. I don't think I'd ever seen him that upset. Watching him as he paced back and forth in our garage smoking furiously, he finally spoke. "Our marriage isn't working and you deserve more than I could ever give you. I think that getting divorced is the only fair thing to do. I can't be the husband that you need or that you want. I want you to be able to find a man that can be all those things to you, but it's not me."

"Why did you marry me?" I said choking on my fear.

"Because I wanted to be the man you wanted, but I know that's just not who I am. I don't actually want children and I know they're important to you," he stammered.

"I don't need to have children. I love you and I'm married to you," I cried.

"It's more than that," he said pacing and smoking. "I'm stressed out by the dogs and it's difficult for me just to come home at the end of the day."

Crying, I just sat there, not sure what to say. He continued, "I don't want to go out to dinner or go to the

28

movies or take trips together. I think I was meant to live the bachelor lifestyle and I just wasn't cut out to be a husband."

"You're a great husband," I argued, worrying that his insecurity was causing him to see our relationship in a way that it wasn't.

"Karen," he said, looking at me with deep sadness in his eyes. "I'm not."

"Yes, you are!" I yelled at him, trying to stop this conversation. "We just need to work harder. We can do it. We can have the marriage we want."

"No, we can't," he said flatly. Looking at me with tears in his eyes, he adds, "I think I'm probably gay. I love you so much and I need to set you free so that you can have the life that you deserve."

Bewildered as I stared at him, I couldn't comprehend what he was saying. He *wasn't* telling me that our marriage was over. I *wasn't* hearing that. I didn't believe that he could be gay. We did have sex even if it was infrequent. He pursued me and married me...those weren't things a gay man would do. I couldn't comprehend what was making him say these things, but I wouldn't accept them as true. When I was finally able to speak, I said, "I love you. I want a life with you. Our love is strong enough to make anything work. Do not give up on this."

Tears trickled down his face as he tried to get me to stop fighting him. He simply said, "Love is not enough."

Stunned, I didn't know what to do. I wasn't expecting this and it felt like I ran into a brick wall going 100 miles per hour. Words failed me. Shock enveloped me.

Standing up, I walked to the bathroom, shut the door and turned the shower on. I stripped my clothes off and collapsed in the tub, sobbing uncontrollably as the water beat down on me. What the hell was I going to do? My sobs turned into wailing. The pain felt like more than I could bear and I didn't know what to do with it.

"It's going to be okay," he said from the other side of the shower curtain.

"It is not going to be okay if we're getting divorced," I screamed. I was hyperventilating at this point.

He picked me off the shower floor and hugged me. "Please stop crying, please," he begged. "Just breathe. You need to take a deep breath."

I took two long breaths as I sat there naked, soaking wet in his arms. As the hyperventilation subsided, he wrapped a towel around me and turned the water off. The pain was too much for me to deal with, so I went into a numb state. My eyes glazed over and I wouldn't speak.

"Come on," he said gently, guiding me out of the bathroom and over to our bed. Sitting on the edge, I felt paralyzed. Nothing more to say, he walked out of the room. The phone kept ringing in the background while I was trying to process everything. I could hear all of the "congratulations" and "happy anniversary" messages being left by our family on the answering machine. Everyone said they hoped we were out having a romantic night celebrating. Tears streamed down my face as I sat on my bed alone, wrapped in a towel not knowing what the hell to do.

After the initial shock wore off, I threw myself completely into denial. We were *not* getting divorced. He was just lacking confidence and needed reassurance in his ability to be a husband. Maybe I hadn't been nurturing enough. Maybe I hadn't expressed my feelings enough. If I could just make him feel how much I loved him, then he would know that he was all that I needed. I didn't need someone else, I needed him. I told him why I thought he felt the way he did and said that I refused to accept the idea that divorce was the best decision. My view was that we needed to focus more on our relationship. I ignored his admission that he was probably gay, choosing not to think about it. He didn't actually say that he *was* gay just that he thought he might be. Obviously, he had issues, but I was certain that being gay wasn't one of them. There had to be another reason why he said those things.

For the next couple weeks, we tried to act like our marriage was fine and I did my best June Cleaver impersonation. I rationalized that talking about divorce made us realize how much we loved each other and valued our marriage. Even though it was excruciating for us to discuss, I believed that the higher purpose was going to be bringing us back together and making us even stronger. I had to believe that. The alternative was just too horrible.

He went out of town for business for a few days and when he came back, he had that sad look in his eyes again. I couldn't bear to look at him, not wanting to see the pain deep inside of him. The truth was too terrifying to acknowledge. I tried to act like I didn't see the change because I wanted my marriage to work and I wanted to spend my life loving this man and creating our life together. Giving up was not an option. Failing was unacceptable. Instead, I tried to pretend like everything was fine even though I was scared that it wasn't. I did my best to avoid a serious conversation, but eventually it happened.

"Pretending like everything is fine, is not the solution," he said gently. I wish it was that easy to fix but it isn't."

"Please, don't do this," I begged. "I'm happy with our life even though it isn't the life I thought we were going to have. I'm happy as long as I have you."

"No you're not," he said with a sigh.

"Yes, I am," I insisted.

"Karen," he said exasperated, "I just need some time to think."

"Okay," I agreed, grabbing onto whatever shred of hope there might be.

"I can't do that with you here though," he said.

"Do you want to go rent a room for a week?" I asked.

"I don't want to be anywhere else. I need to be here," he said shaking his head. "I need you to go home to your parents for a few weeks."

"But I have a job," I argued.

"I know," he said. "But, I can't see any other option."

"Okay," I agreed, not wanting to push it any further. I could give him time. It meant divorce wasn't a done deal yet. But the thought of calling my parents to tell them I needed to come home was horrifying. It was my home too and I didn't want to have to leave. Sickness hit my stomach at the thought of listening to other people's advice. I just wanted to love my husband. Why was that too much to ask for? If I went to my parents' house, there was a slight chance that we could work through this craziness but if I didn't go, I knew there was no hope.

Shaking and sweating, I called my parents to tell them I needed to come home. They told me running away from my problems wasn't the solution. All I could tell them was that I wasn't running away, that I was doing the only thing I knew to do in order to save my marriage by honoring my husband's request for space and time to figure things out. Reluctantly they agreed, even though I didn't tell them any of the details. I packed my suitcase; I packed up the dogs, and I drove to my parents' house the next day. I was very aware that this would forever change my parents' view of my husband, but I was bound and determined to keep the damage to a minimum. As they asked questions, I tried to shoulder half the blame for the situation and I only said kind, loving things about him. Shutting down my emotions, I walked around like a zombie. Twice I cried and they were short bursts at night when I was alone in my room. I couldn't let my parents see the pain I was going through. I couldn't risk them hating my husband, so I kept it all to myself.

Three weeks had been our agreed upon length of stay. My husband never called me. I knew he wouldn't call the first week but I thought he'd call sometime during the second week to tell me to come home. He didn't. When we were in the third week, I braced myself and made the call. As soon as I heard his voice, I broke down crying so hard that I couldn't catch my breath. He tried to soothe me and I knew that it hurt him to hear me so upset. I told him that I was offered some contract work and was planning on coming back a few days earlier than expected. Since I hadn't heard from him, I was not expecting a positive outcome. He said that he hadn't given up complete hope. Hearing those words recharged my enthusiasm and renewed my drive to save our marriage. If there was so much as a shred of hope, I was going to do everything and anything to make it work.

My family and the few friends I had told were hesitant about us working through things. They didn't think that we wanted the same things and that I'd be happier if I wasn't married to him. Annoyed by their pessimism, I had no use for their opinions. I just wanted to go back home and be with my husband. This was my chance to make it work and I was willing to do whatever I had to do in order to avoid getting divorced. It didn't matter what the cost. When I got home, I could see his exhaustion and his weariness. I, on the other hand, was energized and positive. I'd show him that we could succeed at making our marriage work. He reiterated all of his reservations and said that divorce was in my best interest, but I refused to hear what he was saying and reminded him of the hope he said he still had. If he wanted me to accept a divorce, there were two things he needed to do. He needed to tell me that he wanted it, instead of saying that it was what was best for me. He also needed to take my engagement ring and wedding ring off my hand to signify the breaking of our wedding vows. He wouldn't do either.

We also didn't resume a married lifestyle. We were at an impasse. He wouldn't insist on a divorce and I wouldn't accept that it was the best decision. Over the next year, I'd oscillate between accepting the idea that our marriage was essentially over and trying to find any shred of hope that we could reconcile. Believing in the power of positive thinking, I started writing affirmations that our marriage would survive and prosper. If I could believe hard enough, I could will my marriage to work. What I didn't realize at the time was that I was essentially trying to control my husband by willing him to be someone he wasn't. I wanted him to be the husband I dreamed about, the husband that would be happy in our marriage. I wanted to believe that when he said that he was probably gay, it was just a tactic to push me away and that it wasn't actually true. Refusing to think about any negativity, I ignored it and blocked it out of my mind. Instead, I focused on the relationship we'd had while dating and tried to figure out how to get back to that.

He oscillated over the divorce as well. At times, he would say that he needed more space and that he hoped he'd be able to come back to me and offer me the life I wanted. He even said that he could see us working through everything and having a family together. Every time he expressed his wavering sentiments, it fueled my determination to stay dedicated and committed to our marriage. I refused to accept that we were not compatible as husband and wife. I believed that hard work and compromise would create compatibility. I was wrong.

It took a long time for me to let go. I had a death grip on our marriage. Even though we were no longer living as husband and wife, I believed that our love could somehow bring us back together. I didn't know how I could feel such complete and total love for someone and still not be able to create a successful marriage with them. That made no sense to me. It didn't matter whether it made sense or not because I was heading toward divorce regardless. It felt like everything was speeding out of control and I couldn't stop it.

I felt desperate to find someone, anyone who understood what I was going through. I searched book after book in Barnes & Noble and stayed up late at night googling. One night, I stumbled upon a message board for young women going through a divorce. This was the most difficult and lonely time of my life but now I wasn't alone. There were other women, just like me who were going through this too. There was a huge sense of comfort in knowing that other people "got" me.

A question still loomed over me though. If my marriage was really ending, what was I going to do with the rest of my life? How was I going to go on? I had no answers. I just knew that somehow, I'd have to find a way. The past couple years had been spent completely focused on my marriage, trying to make it work. Without that, I felt lost and terrified. Divorce happens to other people. It wasn't supposed to happen to me. We shared a deep love and commitment. We were best friends and genuinely liked each other. I gave everything I had to my marriage. I opened myself up completely to him and allowed myself to be emotionally vulnerable with him. I had never allowed anyone to get that close to me, but I wanted and needed him to know me and understand me. In the end, none of that mattered because it just wasn't enough to make it work or to keep him from walking away. It wasn't enough to make him not gay.

Finally, I reached a point where I was able to say that I had accepted that our marriage was over and I was ready to move ahead with the divorce. He never said that he wanted a divorce. It wasn't that I wanted it either. It became my need for closure, my need to end some of the suffering and my need to start healing that motivated me to initiate the divorce proceedings. He seemed comfortable letting things sit in limbo indefinitely. When I realized that our marriage was completely over, I believed that it was out of our deep love for each other that we needed to set each other free and so I took control of the situation and filed the paperwork.

Reeling from the devastation of losing my husband, I couldn't bear the thought that I'd lose my best friend too. We decided that no matter what, we'd be fair and good to each other through the divorce and we would always protect our friendship. There were a lot of tense moments and a lot of emotions as we dealt with the separation of our lives. We were interwoven together and I couldn't imagine how either one of us would be whole again after we'd torn ourselves apart. I wouldn't allow myself to think poorly of him and I didn't say anything negative about him. I rationalized and justified his behavior and treatment of me and I refused to blame him for anything or hold him accountable for his actions. The most I would say was that our marriage just didn't work. I felt a need to protect him and to keep other people from thinking less of him. Refusing to acknowledge any anger that I felt, I focused instead on trying to maintain the love that I had felt for him. In retrospect, I think avoiding the anger was the only way for me to make it through each day. I couldn't process what was going on so I created a scenario that wasn't as painful and continued to avoid any thoughts about my ex being gay.

Initially, I felt like going through a divorce made me a failure. I felt awful about myself and awful about my ability to be a wife. Something must be wrong with me if I couldn't make my marriage succeed. I was embarrassed, ashamed and horrified that I wasn't yet 30 and I was about to be divorced.

What was even more horrifying was that a gay man had actually married me.

Slowly, I realized that I was accepting society's view of divorce and I was accepting their label of a failure. I was free to either keep accepting these views or I could reject them, choosing to create my own view of my situation instead. Choosing to reject society's view of divorce helped empower me and led to me feeling better about myself.

My divorce was a powerful experience where I learned about life, love and loss. I gave everything I had to my marriage and it wasn't enough. I accept that or at least I try to. Forgiving yourself for making a commitment of marriage that you couldn't live up to takes time. I will always love, honor and cherish him. It just won't be in the context of a marriage. It took a tremendous amount of courage for me to file for divorce. If I had tried to stay married to him, my soul would have been smothered. Instead, I honor my soul and am pursuing bringing my true self to light. Through my divorce, I now have an opportunity to do that. I feel like the best thing I can do for myself at this point is to take every ounce of positive energy from my experience and leave all of the pain, hurt and disappointment behind. Some days I succeed at maintaining this perspective and other days I continue to feel like a horrible failure but each morning I return to the same goal, knowing one day it will simply be automatic.

The judge reads out my married name, which snaps me back to the present moment. As I stand and walk forward, I realize that was the last time I will be legally known by this name. She reviews my paperwork and confirms the information. Then she signs off on my divorce. It's over in approximately 60 seconds. Collecting my signed and stamped paperwork, I turn toward the door. Half the courtroom has emptied out and the other half is waiting their turn to receive their official divorce decrees. A sense of relief washes over me. It's finally done. I can breathe. Instead of sadness, I feel a sense of happiness. It surprises me. I now have my freedom and I hope that both of us can find closure and peace. Going through a divorce was a very traumatic experience, but I survived and now it's time for me to finally rest.

The past four years were exhausting and it took a lot out of me. When I finally allowed myself to get off the sinking ship and swim for shore, I felt liberated. I refused to continue sacrificing myself and instead decided to start living for me. After getting the divorce behind me, I feel ready to embrace life again. Everything seemed so bleak and gray for so long and now there's happiness and color starting to pop back into my world.

When I first started having the divorce talks with my ex-husband, I couldn't imagine life without him. I couldn't imagine dating other men and heaven forbid being intimate with other men. It didn't seem possible that there would come a time when I didn't feel like his wife. But, all those things came a lot quicker than I had expected. Once I made the decision to file for divorce, I felt completely done with that part of my life. I was ready to move forward and I was ready to explore new possibilities for my life. The hardest part of getting divorced was letting go of the future I had planned and envisioned with my ex-husband. Letting go of what we actually had wasn't that difficult. It's exciting to know I have a second chance and there are limitless possibilities waiting for me. I only have to think about myself now. I don't have to consider what my ex-husband wants or be impacted by his actions. I am free to make all of my decisions on my own and to live my life the way I choose to.

The months prior to my divorce, I spent a lot of time alone. Giving myself time to reconnect with what I wanted, who I was and who I wanted to be, and heal; I felt cocooned. During this transition I needed to withdraw and focus exclusively on myself. I didn't want to have a fling or a rebound relationship. Instead, I wanted to enter dating when I felt ready and when I felt like I had a clear head. During my time alone, I read a lot self help books, Oprah magazines and did a lot of self-exploration. I learned how to enjoy being alone and enjoy the new life that I had. Despite spending a lot of time alone healing, there were things that I knew I couldn't heal by myself. Because of the amount of rejection I felt in my marriage, I felt very unattractive and undesirable. My husband had no sexual interest in me the whole time we were married and he was intimate with me only when he felt guilty and only because he felt obligated. I felt like it was somehow my fault or that there was something wrong with me that made him avoid any and all intimacy. I still felt that way even after his admission of being gay. What could be so wrong with me that a gay man would marry me? Even though I worked on rebuilding my self-esteem, it wasn't until I was around men that found me attractive and desirable that I started to let go of that negative view of myself. For me, healing has been a continual process, and one that I'm still working through. It feels more like a journey than an end point destination.

When I started dating again, it felt strange and awkward. I used to be someone's wife. Now I'm someone's date and one day, I will be someone's girlfriend. It seems so juvenile and silly after being married. And yet, that's the dating process. I know that I want to get remarried one day and so, this is what I have to do to eventually get to that point. My first date was right before my divorce was finalized. I didn't feel comfortable dating even in a casual way until I had filed my divorce paperwork because I still felt committed to my marriage vows even though my marriage had disintegrated a long time before then.

Adjusting to dating hasn't been easy for me. It's actually pretty terrifying. After having my marriage end, I feel extremely vulnerable. I'm scared to let someone get that close to me again. I'm scared that I'll give everything I have to another person and it won't be enough. Can I handle the disappointment and heartache of having yet another man walk out of my life? Logically, I tell myself that if the relationship isn't working, then it's not right. It's about compatibility and isn't a personal failing. No matter how sound of an argument that seems, it's still difficult to believe and trust.

I know that if I want to have a relationship at some point, I'm going to have to allow myself to be vulnerable and really express my true self instead of keeping up an iron wall. I share very little personal information and avoid discussing emotional topics. I don't want to feel too exposed. I'm also afraid of telling men what I want. I'm concerned that they will give it to me, but that it won't be genuine and it will only be an illusion that will inevitably vanish. To avoid this, I don't express my desires at all and I don't ask for anything. I'm trying to reach that point that I can trust again and feel comfortable expressing myself. I know that the men I go out with aren't my ex and deserve a chance to get to know me but it's hard. I find myself sabotaging things to keep the men at arm's length or to force them out of my life before they have a chance to leave me on their own. I'm conscious of these behaviors and I want to overcome them. Finding a way to let go of these fears is necessary if I want to be in love again. At the moment, I don't know how to get there. I hope in time I'll find my way.

Anger towards my ex-husband has been slowly building since I've been divorced. I tried to be loving and kind throughout the separation and divorce. But now I realize that I ignored my anger and never dealt with it. It's coming back and I have to start experiencing it in order to move forward. The men that I've gone out with since the divorce have been kind and thoughtful and have wanted to spend time with me and do things with me. How can these men that barely know me want to do all these things that my ex-husband found so impossible to do? How can I get treated better by some of these men than by my own husband? It makes me sad and it makes me angry. Instead of fighting the anger, I'm acknowledging it and letting it come and then watching it fade. It's an unpleasant part of the healing process but necessary.

My ex-husband portrayed himself during the months we dated as someone that he wasn't. He pretended to be the kind of man that I was looking for, the kind of man that I wanted to spend my life with. I know that part of him hoped that he could transform himself into that man for me. But, his lack of honesty over who he truly was is hard for me to deal with at times. I feel like I was conned and that my marriage was a sham. If he had stopped pretending that he wanted the same things in life that I wanted and shared with me who he really was, I wouldn't have married him. His lack of honesty took four years of my life and put me through an emotionally devastating divorce. I put everything I had into a marriage that was doomed from the start. He didn't put me through this out of malice. He genuinely wanted to be the husband I wanted, but that was an impossible dream. I remind myself that I am allowed to feel whatever I feel and it's okay if I'm angry sometimes. One day the pain and the anger that currently bubble up from time to time will dissipate completely.

As I'm driving home from work on a warm summer day, I find myself reflecting on how quickly my life has been transformed. It's been almost two years since we started discussing divorce and six months since our divorce was finalized. Even though I'm still processing all of my emotions from my marriage and my divorce, my focus is on creating a life I want for myself. My new job pays the bills and I don't really mind going to every day. I'm writing in my spare time and working on finishing a novel. The bond that I have with my family is stronger now than it ever has been. When I was moving out of the home I shared with my husband, I dreaded telling them that I was going to get divorced. My parents had been married for 30 years at the time and I was afraid that they would be disappointed and think that I hadn't worked hard enough at my marriage and simply gave up. One day while I was on the phone with my Mom, I just blurted it out. Then I cried hysterically because I was so ashamed. My parents surprised me and actually felt like getting divorced was the right thing to do and that it was in my best interest. They knew something was really off about our marriage even though I couldn't bring myself to tell them the ultimate reason for my divorce. Admitting his sexual identity issues to myself was difficult, let alone sharing that with anyone else.

My parents offered their love and support and did everything they could think of for me. It meant a lot that my family rallied around me. My friendships have been vital to me during this transition also. I'm going out and doing fun things that I never did when I was married. I've been to movies, concerts and parties, and have been hiking several times. When I want to go out to dinner or out for drinks, I have friends who are happy to join me. It amazes me that life can change so much in such a short amount of time.

It's late in the afternoon when I pull into my empty parking spot. I turn off the radio and the air conditioning. For a moment, I sit in the quiet looking at the townhouse in front of me. Then as I turn off the ignition and climb out of the car, a smile spreads across my face. I'm home. I'm finally home. Unlocking the door with my key, my dogs race down the stairs to greet me as I step inside. We exchange hellos as I pet them and they offer me welcome home kisses. A few minutes later, the three of us are bounding out the door, heading for our daily walk. I'm settling into the townhouse I just bought and am having fun decorating it while I'm working toward paying off the credit card balance from my marriage. As we walk through our new neighborhood, I can't help but smile again. I'm happy; really, really happy. The tears have dried, the emptiness has fallen away and the ache is gone. I never thought I'd make it through a divorce. There were moments that I thought the pain might kill me and moments when I wished it would. But it didn't and I'm really proud of myself for being able to triumph over it. I feel stronger, more independent and more alive than ever. This second chance is one that I'm extremely grateful for and embracing. I don't know where my life is headed, but I'm determined to make the best of it and enjoy the journey. Reaching down, I pat Bailey and Sierra. Life is good.

Sleepless in Chicago

By: Michelle Nicolet

"Wake up, wake up," I kept telling myself but no amount of prodding was going to return me to the happily ever after world that I thought I resided in. Unfortunately, I had to start facing the facts that I was separated and headed for divorce regardless of how shocked I felt. People always say there are signs and, I suppose, in retrospect, my marriage wasn't as perfect as I had believed, but my husband's announcement on that cold November evening stunned me, propelling me into this nightmare I felt desperate to escape.

Up until that point, I would have bet on my life that he would never leave me. We had always had one of those relationships our friends envied. It felt like a fairytale and he even called me "Princess." My heart aches when I think of how tenderly he treated me. He used to insist on picking me up and driving me home whenever we had a date so he wouldn't worry about me driving home late at night. When we would fall asleep cuddling on a cold Chicago evening, he would wake up and go outside to warm up the car at ridiculous hours in the morning before I had to go home. After a long day, he used to massage my feet or run me a bath. Always considerate of my needs, he was there for me whenever I needed him. I loved him dearly and I knew he loved me.

After six years of dating, I felt completely secure in our relationship when we married. At that point, I was 24 years old; he was 25. We were friends in high school for several years before we started dating in college and were inseparable. After taking some courses at a community college, we transferred together to an out of state school and got an apartment. I remember being so excited to move in together. We had always gotten along really well, sharing a goofy sense of humor, solid values and similar family backgrounds. For some couples, living together is the ultimate challenge. Dealing with each others habits day in and day out can be quite a shock, but, for us, the transition was easy and felt like yet another sign that it was meant to be.

After graduation, we moved back home to Illinois and in with our respective parents to save money. He proposed on our fifth anniversary with a sweet letter in a bottle. We bought our house that spring and married the week of our sixth anniversary in a Jamaican beach side ceremony. I was so excited to start our lives together with our new jobs, our new house and our new marriage. Looking back, I wish we would have spent more time focusing on each other and our relationship, but I thought our relationship was strong and I was sure it would always be.

A month after we married, I enrolled in graduate school while my husband was working his way up the corporate ladder in a high stress job. I was still working full time in addition to going to school, so I didn't have a lot of free time, but whatever time I had, I always spent it with my husband. The first year of marriage went by pretty quietly. We made all household decisions together, shared bills, and even did grocery shopping together. We were both fairly exhausted every day due to our schedules, so after dinner we would collapse in front of the television. The weekends usually went by in a blur of schoolwork and household tasks. It was a busy time but I felt happy knowing that we were building our life together.

As was the case throughout our entire relationship, we rarely fought. Just after our first anniversary, there was, however, a bit of tension in the house. I was having a difficult semester at school which demanded even more time than usual. While I was busier than ever, he had just been promoted and the dynamics at work had changed so he had more free time. We had a few arguments about me not being as available as he would like me to be, but nothing drastic. Not wanting him to wait around for me, I was supportive of him spending more time with friends, hanging out in the city and having fun. I felt guilty for not having more time to be with him, but I figured it was a temporary situation; one we could ride out. He had always been supportive of me going back to school and I knew things would get better once I graduated.

Doubts about our relationship never entered my head, not even when we began having problems being intimate with each other. For a couple of years, this area of our relationship had become a sore spot. I wasn't very interested in sex, but attributed it to stress, as well as, the normal waning of passion in every relationship. At one point I asked my doctor about it, but my concerns were brushed off. I reasoned that what we were experiencing was normal and that we couldn't expect it to be the same as it had been when we were first together. My husband and I talked about the situation from time to time and I thought we had a mutual understanding. I loved him with all my heart - that had never changed - and he loved me.

Our sexual issues did not seem very important in the overall scheme of things. On a daily basis, it didn't change the fact that we were still a loving couple.

Then one night, we had an extremely frustrating experience trying to be intimate. I just couldn't get into it and we ended up in an argument where we both cried and shared our disappointment. I wish we would have been able to console each other, but no matter what I said, I couldn't make it right. I knew he was taking it very personally and I didn't know how to fix it. I couldn't understand why I didn't enjoy this aspect of our relationship as I once had, but I never doubted our love or the fact that we would get through it. Over the next week, I attempted to broach the subject again, but he wouldn't talk about it and wanted to let it go. We moved on and the next time we were intimate, all seemed fine. Life returned to how it had been and that's how we continued for the next several months.

We squabbled a bit more than we used to and I noticed him being distant, but I attributed it to my own moodiness and my stressful time at school. "If I can just get through my Master's program, things will get better," I thought. His outings with friends started to become more frequent, which didn't bother me at first. But then, he made plans to go out on a weeknight. This was unusual, but there was some occasion at work so I figured it was okay. When he didn't come home by the time I expected him, I worried, but waited. Not knowing whether I should be scared or mad, I called his cell phone. There was no answer. Eventually, I fell asleep after going through all kinds of dramatic scenarios in my head involving horrific car crashes. Trying to calm myself down, I reasoned that he was probably just having fun and lost track of time. I was upset that I couldn't reach him, but what could I do? My eyes grew heavier as I watched the door, waiting for him to get home until they finally closed and I fell into a restless sleep.

When he came home and got into bed, I rolled over and saw the time. My body stiffened and I just lay there fuming, barely saying a word to him. He later apologized and I accepted, but I had a nervous feeling in the pit of my stomach. I didn't like his attitude or behavior. Still, he had apologized and had never acted like this before, so I let it go.

We still did the same things we always had done together, sharing dinner, grocery shopping and watching TV. He kissed me every day before leaving for work and told me he loved me, but I could sense the distance growing between us. There was an unspoken tension that made me uncomfortable. Then one night at Wendy's, it finally came to a head. We were at the drive-thru and I wanted him to ask the lady at the window if they still had a certain chicken sandwich special. The sound was muffled through the speakers and the

54

lady couldn't understand him. He repeated the question several times, but with no success. "Just pick something else," he seethed but I suggested we go inside. He blew up and swore at me. He had never spoken to me this way in our entire relationship. I realized something was very, very wrong. I knew this fight had nothing to do with chicken sandwiches. "What the hell is the matter," I yelled back and burst into tears, crying all the way home while he sat in silence.

When we arrived home, I didn't want that stupid chicken sandwich anymore. I went straight upstairs to the bathroom, closed the door and sobbed. He tried to coax me out, but I stayed in there for nearly an hour. When I eventually came out, we sat down on the couch together. We proceeded to have an argument that I couldn't quite comprehend and then he said, "I don't know if I want to do this anymore." When I asked what he meant, he replied flatly, "be married." Wanting to die right then and there, I collapsed, feeling completely inconsolable. My heart had just been ripped from my body.

He waited for me to calm down, we talked some more but I was numb and can't remember what was said. I just know I cried myself to sleep that night. That was the week of Thanksgiving and the next couple days leading up to the holiday were horrible. We barely spoke until the night before

Thanksgiving. The conversation was the same. He didn't want to be married anymore. I cried; he cried. Not able to stand the thought of sharing the same room and the same bed, I announced that I was sleeping on the couch. "You don't have to do that," he said, "please come upstairs." When I shook my head, sadly refusing to go, he went to get me blankets. Even as he was ripping my heart out, he was still trying to take care of me.

After another restless night of sleep, I packed a bag and arrived at my mom's house for Thanksgiving dinner, without my husband. Tears poured down my face as I told my mom and my sister what had happened. They consoled me, saying it was surely some form of temporary insanity and that we would work it out. Though I was a jumble of emotions, I missed him terribly already and I convinced myself that they were right. Despite the warning signs I felt certain that we would work through this. I vowed to do whatever I could to save my marriage.

Full of optimism, I returned home after the holiday weekend hoping that my husband had come to his senses and would want to save our marriage. "I know our problems are urgent and I'm committed to doing anything and everything to get our relationship back on track," I told him confidently. Of course, I had noticed the tension between us and knew something was going on, but divorce had never once entered my mind because I believed so strongly in our love. Even now, I trusted that our love would get us through this. He was not so convinced. "I think we should separate," he said, standing his ground. Suddenly an anger I hadn't seen before came pouring out of him. I wanted so badly to reach out, but he wouldn't listen to me. He kept telling me over and over again that we needed to separate. Exhausted, I finally agreed to go stay with my mom for a while, hoping that some space would show him the error of his ways and give us both some much needed time to think. Even though I didn't really want to go, he was adamant and I knew he needed to cool off.

The next month was spent between my mom's house and Barnes & Noble where I read everything I could get my hands on about relationship problems and avoiding divorce. With the help of these books and some more conversations with my husband, I began to make more sense of what he had been feeling and how things had gone wrong. With my daily and weekly revelations, I became more hopeful that we could overcome our problems, but my husband continued to stand his ground.

No matter what I suggested, he remained adamant that the only answer was divorce. Our problems were proof that we weren't meant to be together, he reasoned. When I suggested couples counseling, he replied that therapy was for people who were "messed up" and refused to go. Feeling devastated, I cried; I begged; I pleaded. His family tried to talk to him, but nothing worked. Desperate to find a way to save my marriage, I decided that this separation wasn't working and I needed to move back home with him immediately.

As soon as I came home, he started spending less and less time at the house, choosing instead to stay with his friends in the city. My optimism slowly faded but I stubbornly held on, refusing to let my marriage go so easily. When he wanted to discuss the formal paperwork for a divorce, I wouldn't entertain the idea. My only hope was time so I kept stalling. I thought he might come to his senses and I wasn't going to give up until at least six months had passed.

Days turned into weeks and weeks turned into months. Those six months were excruciating for me as the hope for my marriage started to slip between my fingers. As I slowly came to terms with the fact that my husband had, in effect, abandoned me, I sunk into a depression. How could our relationship come to this? My best friend had become a stranger overnight. After that night in November, when I slept on the couch, we never returned to sleeping in the same bed and the loneliness was most profound at night.

Prior to this forced separation, I had never really been alone. Growing up, I shared a room with my sister. When I moved out of that room, I moved into an apartment with him.

Now, for the first time in my life, I was alone and I found myself waking up in the middle of the night crying; my pillow completely soaked. The silence in our home was deafening. I hated that he would rather sleep on some guy's couch in the city then with me – his wife. Feelings of being pathetic and unloved crashed down on me. In those early days, my best girlfriend would sometimes stay over and sleep in the bed with me. When I would come home from work, I'd always turn the television on just for the background noise. I'd try to watch television, but I couldn't follow the story lines. I'd try to read, but I couldn't focus on the words. Concentrating became more and more difficult even though I craved the distraction. My head was constantly filled with thoughts of my husband, my marriage, and my future and it felt like it was spinning most of the time.

Luckily, that's when I found a message board for other young women going through a divorce. That was my life raft. I wasn't the only one going through this. They were too. Having other women who related to me and knew the pain I was experiencing helped me carry on during these dark days.

Despite feeling overwhelmed, I continued working and was able to maintain straight A's at school. There were many days where I had to shut my office door at work and cry. Driving to work in the mornings, the tears would just spill from my eyes and I kept wondering how I could get through the day, much less the rest of my life without him. I was miserable and angry with myself for being so miserable. My emotions were in a constant state of flux. Some days, I'd have no doubt that I loved my husband, wanted him to come to his senses and realize what he was giving up. Then on other days, I felt so humiliated at the way he had tossed me aside and my pride would kick in. "You don't want to be with a man that doesn't want you," I'd tell myself over and over again. I wavered between the desire to fight for my marriage and the desire to walk away with dignity.

Questions without answers flooded my thoughts. Was I wasting my time? Did he ever really love me in the first place? I was so angry that he could take our vows so lightly and walk away from his commitment. I didn't deserve this treatment and it just wasn't fair. I wanted to hate him, to scream and yell and hurt him like he hurt me. I had dreams where I was hitting and kicking him, but during the light of day I was just sad. I didn't want to let go. I wanted to believe there was a chance. It hurt so much to think that I would never kiss him again, that I wouldn't have his children and that we wouldn't grow old together. My heart kept feeling like it was breaking but I kept holding out hope.

Despite sleeping in separate bedrooms, his clothes continued to hang in our closet. This kept him coming to my room regularly. It wasn't much to hang on to, but it kept him close. After being out with friends one night, I stepped into my closet and my stomach plummeted. Panic flooded my body. He had moved all of his clothes out of our room and cleaned out his drawers. The symbolism of that separation cut like a knife. Tears sprang to my eyes. I knew then, deep inside of myself, that it was over. He was not going to turn around. I went to the closet he was now using, took out one of his shirts and smelled it. Holding it to my face, I sobbed, not wanting this to be happening. It was that night that I realized hope was gone and he wasn't coming back to me.

Clutching his shirt, I prayed that I was wrong and that he would return, but he never did. The reality of that stings even now. Even though I still wanted to believe that there was hope, I also realized I needed to prepare myself for the end of my marriage. At one point I thought about taking a semester off of school. The pain was so great that I didn't know how I would continue, but I found a reserve of strength and forced myself to keep doing everything I had done before. Most nights I took sleeping pills so I could get some rest. During the day, I started exercising. Reaching out to friends, family and a wonderful online support group I found was a huge source of comfort. With the strong emotional support I received, I found the strength to keep going.

Taking care of myself was my priority and I tried to have a little fun to balance out all the pain. It was hard at first, but I dragged myself out of bed and started going out. The period that followed was a very strange, surreal time. On one hand, I started to feel good about myself; I got attention from other men, I enjoyed being out and sociable again, and I started feeling open to new experiences. On the other hand, there was still a constant underlying pain. My husband didn't want to be with me. I had daily moments where I felt completely unwanted, unloved and utterly abandoned. The impending divorce was the first thing I thought about when I woke up and the last thing I thought about when I went to sleep at night. Gradually, these feelings subsided and happier thoughts started to take their place.

As I continued to go out with friends, my confidence was growing. It helped me see that my life would be changing, not ending. I even started to look forward to dating other men even though I had been in this relationship since I was 18. Not having the experience of dating as an adult simultaneously thrilled and terrified me. While I was letting go of the dreams I had shared with my husband and the future I thought I would have with him, I was also opening myself up to a new possibility.

A state of reflection followed. I questioned everything about myself, about love and about relationships. I wondered why my marriage was the one that didn't work when I knew people that had stayed together through worse problems.

After a while, I realized that some questions didn't have any answers and there were some things I would never understand. I began to forgive myself for the mistakes I made and I started sending myself more positive messages. I knew I wasn't the problem. We had both made mistakes. In our case, love wasn't enough, but that didn't mean I was a person unworthy of love. I wasn't being unrealistic in expecting someone to make a lifelong commitment and stick with it. I just hadn't found the right man...yet.

The decision to accept my situation and let go of my husband was a slow, but, ultimately, freeing process. Prior to acceptance, I had moments of intense anger and I constantly questioned why this had to happen to me, but once I moved on to the acceptance phase, I was able to stop all the questioning in my head and forgive him too. Why didn't matter so much anymore. Wanting to move on, did. I started to look forward to the rest of my life and the possibilities before me. I had given my marriage all I could, but now I could let go knowing I had done my best.

After more than six months of separation, I finally agreed that my husband could file for divorce and I wouldn't fight him. The process and the sale of our house would not be complete for another six months. During this time, I still experienced a lot of emotional ups and downs. I started to go days, even weeks without crying, but inevitably something would happen that would upset me. A realization, a memory triggered or seeing a couple walking hand in hand could still bring me to tears. Gradually, these "down" moments became fewer and further between and they were less intense. My good days far outnumbered my bad days and I was hopeful for my future.

Selling our house was an extremely difficult hurdle for me. My mind kept flashing back to the months and days before we purchased the house, when we were filled with such excitement and anticipation. Now it had come to this and I didn't want to deal with the sale at all. Insisting that he work directly with the realtor, I only wanted to be filled in when necessary. By this point, he wasn't living in our house anymore which made things confusing for the realtor, but I didn't care. I stubbornly refused to take part where I didn't have to. Although I accepted that the sale was inevitable, I wasn't happy about it.

As part of my graduate program, I left my job to complete a full time stint as a student teacher. I didn't have a new job lined up for the spring and I knew this meant I couldn't get a place of my own. The only real solution, other than taking time off school, was to move in with my mother. This was less than ideal, but I refused to quit school when I had come this far. After the house sold, I'd move back in but until then, I was going to continue living in our house. The day I came home and saw the big red "for sale" sign in the window caused my heart to sink more than I had expected. When people started coming to the house with their realtors, I cringed. At first, I made sure I wasn't home. At times, this was inconvenient and I became resentful of having to drop what I was doing. Stubbornly I began refusing to leave during these appointments. I don't know why I insisted on punishing myself in that way. Listening to these strangers walk through MY house, making plans for where THEIR furniture would go was a painful reminder that my marriage would soon be over. When they left, I would mock them out loud and curse under my breath. I hated them all.

The divorce would be final in December. My husband was going to go to court but I didn't need to show up. Dread and hope were the simultaneous emotions I had about that day. Inevitable as it was, I still hated that it was happening and still wished my marriage hadn't come to this. Regaining my identity and moving on was a small solace during this time. But the day that I received the official divorce papers from the court with the date that our divorce would be final, was more difficult than I expected. It was a Monday when they arrived in the mail. I knew what the envelope contained, but I didn't want to open it. Sitting on the kitchen counter, it taunted me but I left it there for more than a day, untouched. When I steeled myself to read it, I cried as my eyes glanced over the legal description of the end of my marriage. Who knew when it all started eight years ago, that our relationship would end like this on December 11th? Memories flashed back from those eight years to better days, remembering how much we had once loved each other. The holidays we shared, the lazy Sundays in bed, our intimate moments, our wedding day and the future we had planned flooded me with sadness. I cried for the pain of the last year, for the regrets, for the hurt. I cried with the knowledge that I had to let go and move on – alone.

Eventually, I stopped crying and began to feel somewhat relieved. It was as if a weight had been lifted and I knew I was finally able to move forward. The court date was set for later that week. I thought it would bring another round of tears, even though I didn't have to be present in court, but there were no tears. I went out and had lunch with my mom – and had a large margarita.

I was going to be okay, and felt hopeful and free. The arrival of the paperwork meant that I was now able to reclaim my maiden name. Throughout our separation, I had found "me" again. A chapter of my life was closing, but another chapter was beginning. Our house sold two months later. Friends helped me pack and kept my spirits up. The night before the move, my best girlfriend came to spend the night with me. We toasted with a bottle of champagne to my next adventure.

Moving in with my mother was something I was really dreading. Of course, I love her and we get along fine for the most part, but it was humiliating. The loss of independence was difficult even though I knew it was the best thing to do under the circumstances. After my initial discomfort sleeping alone, I had actually become quite accustomed to having my house to myself. I could eat potato chips for dinner, go grocery shopping only when I felt like it and come and go without having to tell anyone. This felt like a huge step backwards. Three years ago, I had been living with my mom when we got engaged and bought a house together. Now I was divorced, my house was sold and I was heading back home without a job and without a husband. What had happened to my life? It seemed like a really bad joke. Maintaining perspective was what I clung to. At least I had somewhere to go and although I wasn't working, I had enough money in the bank to pay my bills and keep me comfortable. After the whirlwind year I'd had, I realized I needed this time to regroup and process all that had happened. I gave myself permission to relax and take care of myself.

While I continued with school, I decided not to look for a new job for a while. My days were spent reading, thinking and spending a lot of time with friends. Part of me wanted to maintain contact with my ex-husband to see if we could manage some kind of friendship but I decided to take some space from him. We had been able to reach a sort of peace between us prior to the divorce. We both agreed we'd made mistakes, we realized we had both suffered enough and we forgave each other and ourselves. Still, the idea of letting go completely was scary and I wasn't sure I wanted to do it. But, the more I thought about it, the more I realized I needed to separate myself completely from him. I needed more time to heal and redefine my life. Maybe one day we could be friends, but not now.

It's been five months since I moved in with my mother. For the most part, it has been an easier transition than I expected. My mom has been respectful of my need for time and space and has not pushed me to move on. She didn't complain when I took over her family room with all of my boxes and didn't revert to treating me like a teenager either.

Changing my name back to my maiden name was empowering. I was confident that life would go on and, in fact, would get better. The stigma I had initially felt about being labeled a divorcee at 27 no longer mattered. If people couldn't accept it, that was their problem. I know I'm a good person and my ex is a good person and our relationship just didn't work.

Today, I'm hopeful for my future. I graduated with my Master's degree in May and felt really proud of myself for sticking with it through the toughest period of my life. I still feel as if I'm in transition, but I know where I'm headed. My plan is to find a full time teaching position and to move out of my mom's house when I get one. Venturing into the dating world has been interesting and I'm confident that someday I will get married again and have a wonderful future. Savoring the sweet moments in life has helped me to become a calmer, more patient person. The little things don't bother me the way they used to. Having been to a really dark place and survived, I've realized that all difficult times will eventually pass. A greater appreciation for the special people in my life is one of the best things that have come out of my divorce. I'm a better person all the way around. Divorce, although painful, was a turning point in my life. My priorities are in order and my journey has only just begun.

A Conversation with God

By: Michelle Denicola Poole

As a product of a very traditional family, I never imagined that I would be divorced. But, I am and was, within a few months of my third anniversary. Looking back, I spent most of my twenties devoted to becoming the perfect wife, mother and teacher. While striving for perfection, I lost sight of who I was and the fact that no one is perfect.

My parents provided me with a strong sense of my cultural roots. My mom was born and raised in Italy while my father was an early generation American; his father was Italian and his mother Polish. No holiday or celebration in my youth was without a ton of family gathered amongst mounds and mounds of food lovingly prepared by the women of the family.

I am the oldest of three children and the only girl. My brothers and I were raised by both parents whose strong marriage was rare in a time when divorce was commonplace among our friends' parents. My father was the quintessential Dad – the provider, the disciplinarian, the rock. My mother, the stay at home mom, could do anything. If asked it, she could answer it. She did things that most moms didn't. She grew her own vegetables, tended to her hundreds of flowers, made everything from scratch and loved her children with an intense passion few children receive these days. Her life was her family. My brothers are very different from me, each one with their own personality and style. I loved being the older sister and took that role to the extreme at times. I was the voice for one of my brothers for so many years and the other was my "baby." As a teenager, I took him everywhere with me.

Both of my parents have five siblings which make for a large extended family. As a child, I was surrounded by many aunts, uncles and cousins. I'm also the oldest of my 16 first cousins living in the United States and there are also six first cousins in Italy. Being the oldest of many played a significant role in how I defined myself. I felt a sense of responsibility to everyone and felt like I always had to do everything exactly right. If I ever messed up, I felt like I would taint the family name and set a bad example.

In my family, divorce is not prevalent or even discussed. I know that my two oldest paternal aunts were divorced and one paternal uncle was too. As a child though, I never really understood or recognized this. Their lives were never talked about. One aunt and one uncle remarried. The uncle's remarriage ended in a second divorce and that was also swept under the rug. I knew that when I married it would have to last forever and the odds seemed to be in my favor, since the majority of my family had long, successful marriages. My parents struggled in their marriage with typical problems, but I never saw them waiver from the commitment they had made to each other and their love for each other has always been evident. Today, I find myself in constant admiration for what they've been able to achieve together.

My maternal grandparents had a long distance relationship. My grandfather lived in the United States and my nonna in Italy. Even though I only knew them for the first six years of life, I knew they loved each other. Nonna was committed to making my grandfather happy by sacrificing everything for his dreams. She endured living separately. My paternal grandparents were married for more than 50 years. They had a fabulous relationship that relied on trust, humor, devotion and respect. Watching their interactions as a child was inspiring. Grandma knew exactly what Grandpap wanted all the time. Of course there were rocky times, but that never stopped the relationship from growing and developing. When I watched my grandma at his bedside during his last hours of life, I was deeply moved. She held him, talked with him and cared for him in ways beyond belief. Their love was real and intense. My family provided wonderful role models for what marriage should be like and this should have provided a foundation for me to be successful at marriage. Unfortunately, I wasn't able to live up to it in my own marriage.

In a cultural sense, a lot was expected of me as the only and oldest girl in my immediate family. I felt that I needed to be the best at everything. This pressure was something I put on myself, but at times it felt like the world expected it of me. My mom always encouraged me to be better, do better and think bigger. This was her way of supporting me, but I interpreted her words to mean that I was never good enough. She often told me that I should never be like her. She wanted me to strive to be more than a stay at home mom. She wanted me to have a career and be a mom. She wanted me to "have it all."

My parents stressed the importance of education. But for me, school was a threatening environment because I didn't make friends easily and I always felt like an outsider. Even though I wanted to be in the top classes, I tended to fall into the average ones. I felt like I was letting everyone down. Through perseverance, I worked hard enough to make it into the top classes. Pushing myself to succeed, I was an average student achieving above my teachers' expectations and my standardized test scores. I needed to get the A's or I would be disappointed.

Reading is one of my passions and I often used a book to escape the reality of my life. I would fantasize that I was the different characters in the stories and dreamed up new lives for myself. My favorite books were set in historical settings. In my mind, being a pioneer was the ideal way to live because women's roles were very defined and life just seemed simpler. Eventually, I graduated with honors from high school and then college. I was starting to achieve the things I had dreamed of in my youth.

Dating did not come easy to me, either. I never liked the way I looked - feeling too fat, too short, too this, too that. My low self-esteem clearly affected my chances for finding love in high school. There were many offers to go to the school dance, but the relationship wouldn't last beyond the dance. Lying awake at night, I'd wish that I had a boyfriend or even a date and could experience life like my friends. I learned quickly that it took more than a pretty face to keep a boy's attention. Eventually, I dated a boy the summer before my senior year. The relationship ended when he slept with my best friend's sister. Devastated, I shut out two other guys that started showing interest in me and would have been great matches because I didn't want to go through that pain again. My first kiss was when I was 17 years old so you could say that I was a late bloomer.

College dating didn't get any easier for me. Everyone around me was drinking and sleeping around while I had never had a drink or had sex. I hadn't planned on drinking until I was of legal age and sex was out of the question. Vowing to myself early in my life, I promised to be a virgin until marriage. My parents never discussed sex with me and didn't encourage me to take this position. However, I was taught this outlook in my church and that was enough for me. Always doing what I was told, I never questioned authority. When I entered college, I was thrust into a world I didn't understand; one where everyone around me not only questioned authority, but rebelled against it. Despite feeling like an outsider, I survived my college years and was able to stay true to myself, but I met a lot of temptation along the way. Looking back at my experiences with men, I realize I dated sporadically because I never wanted to give anyone the chance to get close to me. Simply put, I was afraid of men.

I'm a Roman Catholic and, therefore, was raised to accept and believe what the bible says and never question what the church tells me to do. At least that was me until I was 27, when I got divorced. I've always loved going to church and I have such admiration for religious life. As a child, Mary, the mother of Jesus, was my strongest role model. She was, in my opinion, the perfect woman and person. I spent a lot of my life dedicating myself to being more like her. While in high school, I remember wanting to be a nun. I seriously looked into convents and believed I had been called twice to this kind of life in dreams. When I discussed my choice with my mom, she laughed at me and said that I could never be silent and modest for so long. She was right, but I was offended and continued to believe that I would make a good nun. I felt it would give me the discipline I thrived on. It wasn't until I was in college that I realized that the vision to be a nun was really an escape and an excuse to cover up my lack of dating experience and to save me from my fear of men. I don't know what caused that underlying distrust of men, but it was there and evident in my dealings with them. To this day, I still love being Catholic and exploring all the beauty of my faith. And, Mary is still a role model for me because of the belief she had in God. She didn't let the choices he made for her waiver her at all, even if it caused her to be an outcast in her family and society. She was a major source of strength for me through my divorce.

I met my former husband during my last semester in college. He was kind enough to help me get my passport renewed for a two week scholarship trip we were both taking. We went on the scholarship trip and the rest, as they say, was history. We spent all of our time together while in London. We toured the city, dutifully studied and began our relationship. When we returned home, he went back to the university to continue work on his masters degree and I returned to my home to student teach. Our long distance relationship was built on daily phone calls that lasted for hours and on spending every weekend together.

The keys to our relationship were communication and family. We spent so much time with my parents that they grew to love him like their own son. My father had so much admiration for him. He was instantly close to my family and developed a strong bond with my father and my brothers. It was as if they were the family he never had.

My former husband's childhood was very different than mine. He's an only child and his parents divorced when he was 10. He lived with his parents and his maternal grandmother until his parents' divorce. When his father left, he was raised by his maternal grandmother, mother and godmother, all of whom lived in the same home. His relationship with his father was inconsistent. He talked to him on birthdays and saw him infrequently when he was younger. Now that he was grown, he saw his father about twice a year. He loved and respected his "mothers" and they always catered to him. He fulfilled the "man of the house" role for all of them. His mother worked long hours during his childhood at a flower shop and she enrolled in college once she was divorced. She continued on in school for the following 10 years until she earned her PhD in counseling education. He always had pets, particularly dogs and fish, and he invested most of his personal time in them. His friends were few, but close and generally shared common interests with him. He was always a gentleman around my family and me, and his reputation was upstanding. Everyone who met him, including my family, loved him.

A few months after we started to date, I completed my student teaching and graduated college. With the blessings of God, I was able to find employment locally. He was still an hour and a half away completing his degrees. We continued with the long distance communication and quickly fell in love. He was amazing and I finally had the boyfriend I had longed for so many nights as a teenager. He completed me and was my angel. I was fascinated by his intelligence and love for anything and everything. If I asked him a question, he always knew the answer or researched the answer and wowed me with what he came up with. He would spend hours with my father helping around the yard or building whatever project Dad was working on. He spent time with my brothers getting to know them and spent special time one on one with each of them, even attending my brother's marching band competitions. Sitting with my Mom, he would ask her questions about her life in Italy or help her in the kitchen preparing a meal. Even more endearing, he was willing to spend the holidays with my family and drive for hours to pick up my brother at college so he could spend the holiday with us, too. Always sacrificing for us; he was a dream come true. Looking back, perhaps he was too perfect.

What delighted me the most about him was his love of the Catholic Church. We attended mass together and he became involved with my church. He helped me lead the youth program and even guest lectured about the history of the church and Jesus with our RCIA groups. We shared the same views on sex and the importance of waiting for marriage. He never pressured me to explore our sexuality and we always talked about how we were intimate in many other ways. We felt our deep conversations, sweet caresses and commitment to each other proved the intimacy and love we had for each other. Our sexual relationship would grow once we were married.

We didn't have many mutual friends, but we spent a lot of time with my friends. We were always around couples and saw many of my friends get married and start lives together. I was starting to feel the itch to be married too.

We had been dating for two years. During that time, it seemed like everyone else's life was moving on around me while I was still living at home, teaching, completing my masters and dating my boyfriend on the weekends. I wanted more. The time seemed right for us to move forward and to start creating more of a life together. He was busy completing his master's thesis and starting his doctorate program two hours away from where he lived. He commuted to his new school and also taught at that university. Our time together on weekends was even more precious because of how busy our weeks were. We had been talking about marriage since the second month we were dating but our talks began taking a more serious tone at this point. Without my knowing it, he had bought me an engagement ring six months after we began dating and had been holding on to it for the past year and a half. He used the money he had been saving for a kayak to buy me that ring. Later on, he told me that he had been trying to ask me to marry him for months, but odd things happened each time he had it planned. Envisioning us getting married the following summer, I started to feel the time crunch to plan it and didn't want to start until we were officially engaged.

Finally, on a random Wednesday summer night date, he got down on one knee in a favorite park and asked me to be his wife. He expressed how much I completed his life and he bought me a special collectible; we had been collecting a series together for over a year. It was entitled "Be my one and only." It was perfect. We immediately went to see my grandparents at their resting places and then my mom at work. When we got home, my father knew and was ecstatic for us. Plans immediately commenced for our wedding the following summer.

My parents were married one month before my mom's birthday and following tradition; I would be married exactly one month after my birthday. We spent the next year creating a special event with the help of my parents. It turned out to be a fairy tale wedding that people still talk about. The memories of that day aren't bitter for me or my family. Now, we think of the wedding as an extravagant family reunion. On July 17th at 3 pm, at the ages of 25 and 27, we entered into holy matrimony with a full Catholic Nuptial Mass. The ceremony was followed with an enormous spread of foods and desserts with partying that lasted late into the night. Our photographer even commented about how impressive the wedding was, saying it was one of the best she ever photographed. Those snapshots just sit in a box at the top of my closet today.

Throughout the detailed planning of our wedding, we never lost sight of the marriage. My fiancé and I never thought the wedding was the only thing to plan for. We took marriage very seriously. His parents were divorced and the events surrounding that were not explained clearly to me. I was determined not to have history repeat itself. We did our Catholic Church Precana work which included meetings with the priest, communication tests and a weekend retreat to focus on our relationship. We made it through with flying colors. I even remember the priest's assistant, who had been working closely with us, raving about how compatible we were together and how wonderful our relationship was and would continue to be. Nothing seemed like it could come between us or our love. My fiancé and I talked about divorce and what possible problems could come up between us, but we always had the perfect answer as to how to solve things. I felt like we'd be immune to divorce.

My extended family loved and adored my husband. He seemed to be instantly a part of the family. At our wedding, my relatives said to him, "It's about time," "Finally, you are part of us," and "We couldn't love you more." In retrospect, I know that he loved this attention and affection he gained from my family. I should have seen that not having a father in his life took a toll on him and that should have served as a warning sign. Instead, I loved that he needed and wanted to spend time with my father and brothers. Because of this, I grew to love him more for taking such an active role in my family.

We married at a good time in our lives. I had been at my job for three years and he was finishing his dissertation the following year. He was working at different universities teaching a class here and there. Our dream was to relocate to the college town where we both completed our undergraduate work. He would teach classes and I would commute to my school about 30 miles away.

Taking on a second job three months after we were married helped with the expenses of living on our own. Neither of us had lived away from home except during our college years. We were learning it all on our own now. He was a wonderful domesticated husband. He cooked, cleaned and led the household during his hours at home. He worked inconsistent hours so he found himself home a lot. I worked a consistent teaching schedule and then additional hours at the local shopping mall. I was popping in and out of our home because I was working an extra 10 to 20 hours a week. Our lifestyle was fairly modest during our marriage. We were able to save a little bit of money, but I was never comfortable with our financial situation.

There were a lot of adjustments we were going through at the start to our marriage. The biggest one for me was being away from my mom, although I talked to her each night and saw her every weekend. It was still difficult to not spend time with her every day. I also was nervous about money, bills, my husband finishing his degree and him finding steady work. His biggest adjustment seemed to be missing his grandmother, with whom he was always with before marrying me. He seemed more at ease with his life when he was first married to me but that slowly deteriorated.

Problems in our relationship started popping up after our first anniversary. His excitement towards his dissertation and degree slowed down and he stopped sharing things with me. He also stopped talking about where he was looking for a job or for what types of jobs he was pursuing. A year and a half into our marriage, he started teaching every night instead of mostly mornings as he had been doing before which meant he was never home when I was. Two months before our second anniversary, I realized our problems were more extreme than I had thought when I discovered he was not going to graduate as planned. My husband didn't share this with me; I learned it from a friend who had called the house while my husband was away on a trip. I excitedly congratulated the friend on his upcoming graduation. Confused, he told me graduation was the week before and that my former husband was not a part of it. I collapsed on hearing that news and knew that our life would never be the same. I had known that things were not right for almost a year, but no matter how much I tried to talk with him about the issues he denied everything. Sensing that this graduation news was just the tip of the iceberg, I had to do something. When he came home two days later, I confronted him with the information I had and the intensity of our discussions turned to an all out fight. We had never really fought, but now it became one constant battle. I spent many nights crying myself to sleep watching my world crumble around me.

All of the problems in our relationship weren't evident to me until it was too late. Once I started noticing them, they began to multiply and before I knew it, things seemed out of control. I tried to talk with him about them, but he wouldn't talk. His solution to most of our problems was to ignore and avoid them and he withdrew from me even more. We worked different schedules and this put even more pressure on our marriage. I worked a lot of hours between my two jobs and he worked many part-time jobs. When he started working only at night, he would not come home until it was very late, claiming he was out meeting with people from school. Around this time, he also started to take "trips" that would last a day or two. During these trips, I didn't know where he was or what he was doing. I would call his cell phone but usually it was turned off, out of range, or not working; according to him. He also started to play hockey on weekends. Desperate to reconnect with him, I asked to come watch him play, but he'd always say no. I felt like he was trying to avoid me at all cost.

Everything we had in common and that had drawn us to each other was disappearing. I wanted children and he no longer did. He refused to even discuss the possibility of children after our first year of marriage. Our love of the church was no longer a priority for him either. What was once the foundation of our relationship was no more. I wanted God and the Catholic Church to be our guide. He refused this after we were married. He became completely apathetic to church and explained that the only reason he ever went was to please me. Eventually, he completely withdrew from me, my family, and even his family, escaping into his work. During this time, I was very emotional and sought his love and support. I wanted him to comfort me and support me when I needed it. He, in turn, shut me out. After he lied to me about not graduating, I was disillusioned, but I was still willing to work on our problems. He didn't seem interested in working on our marriage. He began to make decisions about his future without consulting me. His depression worsened and he refused help.

I didn't share my problems with my family because I knew how much they respected my husband and I didn't want to disappoint them. I begged him to get marriage counseling. He refused for months until he finally gave in and agreed to go. We only attended three sessions because he quickly decided that it wasn't worth his time. I also asked him to meet with a priest to discuss our problems. He adamantly refused to have anything to do with the church. I brought home papers on a Christian marriage encounter and repeatedly asked him to attend with me. He consistently responded that he wanted nothing to do with the church. For all the uncertainty he had in his life, he clearly knew one thing...he did not want to talk about or deal with religion or God. This hurt me the most. How could I save a marriage that had been formed based on our commitment to God and to each other when he no longer had a commitment to either?

That January, he left for a job in Washington, D.C. Going by himself, the plan was that the time apart would be good for both of us to clear our heads and gain perspective on our marriage. He promised to come home often and, in May, I would decide whether or not to move there after my school year ended. After he left, I rarely heard from him. Although we talked sporadically during this separation, I continued to reach out to him, sending letters, emails and care packages hoping to get him to talk to me, open up to me and try to work things out. It didn't happen.

Not long after he left, he called and told me that he didn't plan to ever come home again. Devastated and unwilling to give up, I continued to make efforts to reconcile with him. I wanted to move to D.C. so we could work on our marriage in person but he said no. I asked if I could visit so we could talk about things and he said no. After five months apart with little contact, I'd had enough and told him to make a choice. If he was not coming home and I couldn't be a part of his life in D.C., then he needed to be a man and make a decision about us and our future.

During our separation, I not only made every attempt to reconcile with my husband, but I also used that time to take back control of my life. I had spent the past year or so in such a depression that I didn't know who I was. I entered personal therapy with an amazing doctor who didn't take my excuses as answers to her intense questioning. I would say, "I'm a good Catholic girl. I can't get divorced." She would retaliate with biblical scriptures or advice from her priest friends on how skewed my perspective was. I would say, "We did everything right before we married. We prepared for marriage." Her comeback was that my husband had free will and he made choices that were not healthy in our marriage. She constantly suggested medication to help me sleep and deal with the anxiety and depression I was feeling. I refused any medication, but I did follow a sleep therapy pattern that helped me out tremendously.

During those months, I focused a lot of my energy on my work; throwing myself into my students, lessons and anything that would bring me a moment of peace from thinking about him. Friends and co-workers extended their shoulders, comfort and insight to me. Relationships I had lost because of my stressful married years started to be rediscovered. My extended family had no idea what was going on. My mom was aware that I was going to therapy and that there were issues, but she never knew the extent of them. She and I had made the decision to not share the news of my separation with anyone else in my family. It was embarrassing for her, but, in some ways, we both were holding on to the hope that things would work out and we could just forget about this painful time.

My faith was also renewed and restored during this time. For a person who felt that God was her core, I let all of that go very quickly. While married, I attended church alone many Sundays, but got very frustrated when my husband didn't attend and felt jealous seeing all the happy families around me and so my attendance became sporadic. Despite my sadness about going to church alone, I found the strength to start going regularly again. Choosing a church where no one would know me or recognize me felt like a fresh start and I joined a church group for separated and divorced people. I also sought out the priest's assistant who helped to prepare my husband and me for marriage and discussed our current situation. All of this helped me through my separation and prepared me for what was coming – my divorce.

I grew up believing that divorce was not accepted in the church. But, what I found was that I was embraced and supported by all of the people I consulted from the church. The assistant actually told me I should leave my spouse because of the way I was being treated. I learned that God wants us to be loved in healthy relationships, not fearful ones. When two become one, they must let God enter the relationship. We had not. Pages could be filled of reasons and excuses why our marriage failed, but the bottom line is our marriage was not a Godly covenant. The support group provided me with the comfort of meeting other separated people and divorcees. By the time I received my divorce papers, I was starting to find my way out of the hole my life had become. I was saved by God's graces in a place I had feared being a part of again.

The divorce papers arrived the week before my 28th birthday. He made the decision that he no longer wanted anything or anyone from his "old" life, including me. This new life he had created for himself in D.C. was where he chose to be. Children were not something he wanted and actually had never wanted. His job was now the most important thing in his life and he had no desire to ever be with anyone again.

Tossing away religion and God, he said he was just pretending to believe for me. This was his life now. We were officially over. All my attempts to save our marriage had failed.

The divorce was not contested only because I was exhausted from the constant fight to save my marriage and I, simply, had no energy left. Five months had gone by and I'd only seen him once. We talked on the phone maybe eight times. This man I called my husband was a stranger and I had no idea how to "find" the man I fell in love with and married. Divorce was not something I wanted, but I had no idea how to stop it or how to get my marriage back. It was time for me to stop fighting and start accepting the inevitable, I was getting divorced.

Unable to deny the physical evidence of my divorce papers, I knew I finally had to tell my parents the truth. I visit my parents every Sunday and that weekend I sat on the deck with them and told them that my marriage was over and that my former husband had filed for divorce. My Dad raged, my Mom screamed and I sat up tall and told them I was going to be okay. The relief I felt when I actually received the divorce papers was beyond anything I had felt since my wedding day. My Dad demanded that I not sign the papers yet, to still give it time. I let them have their say but after I left I immediately signed and dated the papers. I couldn't suffer anymore.

The same month I received the divorce papers, I moved into a new, cheaper, more practical apartment. I was ready to start making a new life for myself – one based on my terms. Being a 28 year old divorced professional Catholic woman who had hardly dated before I got married, I was thrown back into being single. Finding a healthy stable relationship was what I desired so I found my courage and ventured back into dating. It was time for the insecure, uncertain girl I had been to become a confident, strong woman in order to find real love. It takes two to create a marriage and two to destroy it. I accept and shoulder my share of the responsibility for my divorce. I'm thankful I didn't shut men out of my life or blame all men for what had happened to me. Instead, I used my divorce as a learning experience and was willing to love again.

While I was beginning to navigate the world of divorce, I found an internet support group of divorced women under the age of 30. I hadn't met one person who was young and divorced until I found this group online. I'm very internet illiterate, but somehow I stumbled upon this amazing group of ladies who could make me laugh and cry and who challenged my views on divorce and life. I finally didn't feel so alone.

The summer my divorce was in process, I treated myself to a vacation with a tour group who specializes in singles vacations. It was an interesting exploration of the

Western States. No one on the tour knew who I was or what had happened in my marriage. I was able to reinvent myself as a single woman. One Sunday, I spent time alone walking along the rim of the Grand Canyon. It was early morning and I had a few hours to kill before the bus departed for our next destination. I stumbled upon the Grand Canyon chapel. It's simply an outlook that juts slightly into the canyon. The sunrise was intense and the location was inspirational. In that chapel I had a conversation with God out loud for the first time. Yelling, crying, and pleading with Him to explain why my life had turned out this way, I begged for the strength to accept my fate. Reasonably, I didn't get my answers through words, but through a calmness and weightlessness I'd never before experienced. As I left that spot, a sense that I felt for the first time that everything was going to be okay, really okay.

As the summer wound down, I started getting ready to go back to work as a teacher. Taking my job very seriously, I feel that teachers should be role models for their students. Now that I was coming back to school divorced, it felt like I'd let my students and my community down. Ashamed, I felt very inappropriate and insecure returning to the classroom. I teach in a small school district where I instruct many of my students two years in a row and the students had no idea what I went through in my marriage. I had worked one year as a Mrs. and was about to start the next as a Ms. Feeling that I needed part of my identity back, I returned to my maiden name immediately. The students hardly noticed, but some students were so sweet and innocent, thinking that I had just gotten married. One even brought me a congratulations card not realizing I was newly divorced. Fortunately, my fear about their reactions was much worse than it turned out to be. We all moved forward and it was forgotten.

The Catholic Church requires an annulment to remarry in the church. Many people don't do the process until they're ready to marry again. Choosing to embrace the process, I proceeded to do it immediately after my divorce was final and I'm so glad I made that decision. It required me to ask my family members, three witnesses and myself extensive questions. The questions were daunting and personal, but they gave me an opportunity to gain a new insight into the truth of my marriage. It gave me the closure I was seeking. The process opened my heart to love and to God again. My annulment was fully granted within nine months of my divorce.

Once settled into my new life, I began to set more goals for myself. I decided not to lose sight of my desire to become a mom, I wanted to get married again and find a good man that would be a good husband and father. My outlook on dating was focused on finding the right person for me rather than just dating for fun. Another goal I chose was to meet new people and get my body back into shape. I joined a few sporting activities in my local community, including a volleyball league because I've always loved volleyball. It turned out that the group was mostly older people, but there were a few younger ones. The first few weeks were nerve racking for me because I didn't know anyone and hadn't played in years. But, I was able to settle down and play my game both on and off the court. Within a couple weeks, I made a few wonderful friends and we started going out afterward.

One person in particular caught my attention. I guess I caught his too, because he soon asked me out on a date. We went on our first date a little more than a month after my divorce was finalized. I was terrified to tell him about my past. When I had gone out on dates with other men after my marriage, I just told the truth, but with this man, it felt different. I couldn't just blurt out, "I'm divorced." Wanting to make sure I told him the whole truth, I also wanted to assure him that I don't take marriage lightly. Late into our first date, I shared my story. He was caught off guard and reserved at first, but accepted it. He didn't tell me until later, but the next day he read the Bible searching for strength in scripture to accept my reality. The word of God provided him the revelations he needed. We've been inseparable even since. The relationship hasn't been perfect or easy, but it has been better than my dreams allowed. He's similar to my ex-husband in many ways and he even shares the exact same birthday as him too. Instead of pretending to be what I wanted, this man shows me who he really is.

As my new life began to take shape, I continued to work with the church support group. I even committed to assisting the group. This role required me to be more active in our discussions and to share my heart and soul about what had happened and was happening. It was an opportunity to share my story with others and to help them grow from their tragedies. I truly believe that everything happens for a reason; even divorce. Before my divorce, I was a very intolerant closed-minded person who proclaimed to be a good Christian. Divorce required me to open my heart to different ways of life and the true word of God. While assisting with the group, I was able to show others how special life can be after divorce. We have a chance to learn from what was and recreate our lives and dreams. The group was my mission and my way of giving back. I also benefited from being there because I made new friends and found people who could understand me and what I'd been through.

Even though my life was being rebuilt, there was still something that I hadn't done yet. My extended family still didn't know I was divorced. Even though I was dating and moving on with my life, no one really knew. My parents didn't tell anyone, not even their siblings. When I was out on a date, I would look over my shoulder praying not to run into a family member. I'm sure they had some clues along the way but it had not been discussed. I stopped attending family functions and when they did see me I was alone and my mother always seemed extremely sad. Deciding on the best way to announce my divorce, I decided to send out one of those dreadful Christmas card letters. It briefly explained that I was no longer married, we were no longer together, that I had moved on and that I was with someone better. Period. I had nothing left to explain. After I mailed them out, I held my breath. But, no one asked me a single question or commented on the situation. In some ways, I was relieved, but in other ways I felt ridiculous. They had to have questions. However, my family is very talented at shoving things under the carpet and I had become one of those things. Some of them did express disappointment that I didn't reach out for help while going through my divorce, but my Mom and I had agreed not to share my story. Nothing more was said.

The sadness the divorce would cause my parents and brothers was something I hadn't anticipated. They loved my ex-husband and accepted him into our family. My ex chose to shut them out of his life. They had to grieve that loss as well. While I was healing and moving on with my life, my mother was stuck. She couldn't get over the fact that her baby girl was divorced. By not sharing the difficulties of my marriage with my family, it made the divorce an even greater shock. It was bad enough that their "perfect" daughter messed up her marriage, but for her husband just to leave without saying anything was too much for words. They still don't know everything that happened in my marriage and how it really felt to be in that relationship. I chose to protect them from the truth, but it has made their acceptance of the divorce difficult. Time is healing their hearts and they have come to terms with my new life.

My mom has to deal with the aftereffect of my divorce. She works in a public place in our community and runs into many people who ask her if she's a grandmother yet. She has to tell them no and they follow with the question, why. She responds by telling them her version of the story; one I chose not to hear. Granted, it isn't anyone's business what happened, but she does have to, at the very least, acknowledge that I'm no longer married.

Recovering from and learning to deal with the stigma I created in my mind about divorce, forced me to grow up quickly. It's funny to think that a 28 year-old woman was not grown up, but I wasn't. I lived in a fantasy world of what I believed everyone else was living: perfect marriages, wonderful children, fulfilling jobs, and solid homes. It felt like I wore a scarlet letter D on my chest for the world to judge me.

I wasn't perfect; I would have to face that. Surprisingly, no one judged me though. No one really seemed to care or be fazed by my divorce except my family and me.

The most important lesson I've learned from my divorce is that comfort isn't found in the arms of another. From a young girl who longed to date to a woman who was an unsuccessful wife, I truly thought the only way I could be whole was through being a mom and being a wife. Consequently, my biggest lesson was that I had to learn to love me and to provide comfort to myself. My divorce does not define me; rather, it's a small part of who I have become.

Today, life has moved on. Five years after my first wedding, I'm planning a second one. The man I met on my volleyball league is now my fiancé. We're planning a small and intimate wedding that's church focused.

Getting re-married has made me examine my first marriage more closely so that I can try to avoid making the same mistakes. Looking back, I honestly believe that my first husband wasn't ready to accept the responsibilities of marriage. This is very difficult for me to say because I felt at the time we had done everything right, but I just don't think he was ready for it. He also didn't have role models to show him the ups and downs of marriage. Even though we talked openly before we got married about problems we might have or problems that I saw occur between my parents, he was still convinced that it would be easy for us. He constantly said he would do whatever it took to make me happy, even after I told him it wasn't necessary. He also didn't have any prior girlfriends or long term relationships, not that I did either, but I had dated where he hadn't. His entire future had been planned out when he asked me to marry him. He knew exactly how things would go, but when they didn't, he seemed to fall apart. He isolated himself and withdrew from me and our marriage. With my current fiancé, I feel secure knowing that he had male role models growing up and can succeed when the plan fails. I'm so excited to be marrying a man who fascinates me, challenges me and energizes me to be a better version of myself. He's taught me how to trust and love again.

An Affair to Remember

By: Michelle Joyce

I can recall with extraordinary detail the moment my husband left me for another woman. Like slow motion it replays in my mind. It was December 5th at 11:17 a.m. At that moment, he slammed the front door behind him, climbed into his car and drove away. Slumped on the floor of my kitchen, I sat there staring at the microwave clock. I can remember even the smallest of details like the feel of the wood cabinets pressing into my back, the bright white light coming in from the windows after an early morning snowstorm, the salty taste of my tears as they rolled off my cheeks and landed on my lips, the smell of his cologne lingering long after he had gone and then the sound of silence.

I don't recall how long I stayed on the floor of my kitchen. It felt like hours, but was probably only minutes. As I pulled myself up, I went over to the front door. Knowing he'd be gone, I still hoped to see his car in the driveway. Feeling overwhelmed with desperation, I would have done anything as long as he was still there, still my husband. When I got to the window, all I saw were the remains of his tire tracks. The snow slowly covered what was left and soon any trace that he had ever been there was gone.

As I turned from the door, I surveyed my home. This house was our first dream and it was not supposed to be our last. It was filled with promise; promise of a life that we pledged to each other in God's house. My house, which had once been filled with laughter, was now full of silence. And it was deafening. But it was only there in the silent rooms of my house that I was able to find my way home.

My marriage began like most - with a wonderful wedding. Even though I spent 18 months laboring over the most minute details, I can't recall very much of my wedding. I call it "my wedding" because that's what it was; a day for me to shine. A day to wear the white dress, walk down the aisle and feel like a princess. Never mind the prince. My ex-husband cared little about the details of the actual wedding and reception. There are many brides who find themselves in this situation and it's perfectly normal; however, it felt like there was something more to his indifference. It seemed cold and fearful. Looking back, I think he regretted asking me to marry him about 10 minutes after I said yes. At the time, I couldn't see this. It was onward and upward. I was about to be a princess and I didn't need a prince who cared whether the bridesmaids' dresses were lilac or lavender. All I needed was a prince who was going to arrive at the church on time and say I do.

As much as I loved the process of planning my wedding and treasured the moment that I could walk down the aisle in my princess gown, I really understood the commitment I was making. The time consuming task of the planning the wedding did not take precedence over the planning of the marriage.

When I said to him, "For all the days of our lives," I meant it. The determination I had to make my marriage last was unwavering and stemmed from the desire not to repeat the mistakes of my parents. Only six when my parents divorced, I lived with the effects for years to come. Shared custody meant traveling to my father's house twice a week to spend time with him. Many years later, I watched my sister struggle through a divorce. When I finally married, I knew I was going to be different. We were not going to be the one out of two couples that got divorced.

To assure my success, my husband and I went to pre-marital counseling with the priest who performed the ceremony. We discussed the responsibilities of marriage. We decided who was going to be responsible for the daily chores that sometime interfere with the romantic and passionate side of marriage. I was going to vacuum; he would take out the trash. He would cook; I would clean. We were a match made in heaven, or so I thought.

After six years together, I was sure that we could get through anything that was thrown our way. We had been tested many times in our courtship by interfering parents and the temptations of others. We had survived and I was convinced nothing could tear us apart.

I don't think it's possible to pinpoint the exact moment a marriage begins to fail. It's like a cancer that slowly eats away the cells of your marriage until there's nothing left.

Truthfully, my marriage began to fail even before I met my ex-husband. I was developing patterns in my relationships with men and with myself that would doom my marriage. My life in the year before I met my ex-husband had begun to deteriorate. After having spent 15 years of my life as a classically trained dancer, I was suddenly without a focus. As the result of one bad audition, I was denied admittance to the dance program at my college and for the first time in my life I had no idea who I was supposed to be. In high school, I was "the dancer." Struggling with adjusting to life as a college freshman and dealing with this loss of identity led me down a dangerous path of drinking and partying.

Then I met a man – Mr. Wonderful. Mr. Wonderful and I met my freshmen year in college. He was a senior and so cute. He was friendly, courteous and caring. As I fell in love, I thought I had met the man of my dreams. We dated over the summer between my first and second year of college. It seemed we were a perfect match: I was in desperate need of saving and Mr. Wonderful was looking for someone to save. He was extremely religious and I saw in him what I wanted for myself – integrity, honesty and purity.

The fatal mistake I made with Mr. Wonderful was not taking the time to figure out who I was without dancing and high school. I never took the time to figure out what made me happy. After losing my identity as a dancer, my only focus became partying until Mr. Wonderful came into my life. Then all of my focus transferred over to being Mr. Wonderful's girlfriend. Who was Michelle? I didn't have a clue. I only knew that Mr. Wonderful loved me and that was enough.

Unfortunately, that wasn't enough for Mr. Wonderful. A few months of dating someone who had no opinion and whose only focus in life was making him happy was too much for him. He dumped me after taking me to the beach for a family vacation which left me devastated. It was not your normal college break-up devastation. I felt like my life had come to a complete stop and I wasn't worth the dirt on the kitchen floor I was laying on after he left me. It's funny how I always end up on the kitchen floor after being dumped, but I digress.

Two weeks later we were back in school and I was off to my new job. As I started working, I really thought I was beginning to focus on myself. The job really wasn't a way to improve myself, it was a diversion from the heartbreak and a diversion from the work I should have been doing on myself. I should have been learning who I was independent of a relationship. Time needed to be taken to learn from my mistakes with Mr. Wonderful and to examine the relationship and myself so I wouldn't spend my life with men who weren't right for me. I told my roommate, at the time, that maybe I would be lucky and meet my future husband at my new job. I must have been psychic because I did meet my future husband and future ex-husband, Mr. Rebound.

Meeting a man two weeks after a boy you thought hung the moon dumps you is not a promising start to a relationship. But, I was 19, the age when I knew it all and was sure that my friends and families' words of wisdom were gibberish. The warnings to stay away from men and to focus on myself went in one ear and out the other when Mr. Rebound came into my life.

The general rule of rebound relationships is that they last a few weeks, maybe a month, and fizzle very quickly when you finally come out of the fog that you've been living in since being dumped. Clearly, I was the exception to the rule. My rebound relationship lasted eight years. When I met my ex-husband I didn't realize the weight of the baggage I had been lugging around since my father left my mother 13 years prior.

The reason that clichés become clichés is because they're true. No statement could be truer than - hindsight is 20/20. It's only after years of examining my relationship that I realized the mistakes I made. When you are in the midst of your life, moving forward and watching the weeks, months and years pass, it's difficult to see the problems. It's difficult to see your mistakes. Especially when you know little to nothing about what makes you happy.

Without any real insight into the mistakes I made in the past, I dove head first into a relationship with my ex-husband. We were immediately attracted to each other and in less than a week he made it perfectly clear that he only wanted to date me. This was the validation I had been seeking in my life. For the first time I felt as if I was worthy of being loved. In the beginning, my ex-husband made me feel like I was everything I thought I wasn't - nice, caring, smart and beautiful. His pursuit of me convinced me that Mr. Wonderful had the problem, not me and suddenly I was free of the responsibility over the demise of that relationship. How could someone want me so strongly, if I were so bad? Being free of that responsibility left me feeling like nothing needed to change in my life.

What I didn't know at the time was that Mr. Rebound had issues of his own. There were signs. I was blind to them because I was only seeing what I wanted to see. He wanted to be with me; therefore, I convinced myself that every bad thing I thought about myself couldn't possibly be true. If I had taken the time to learn who I was without a man, I would have learned what I wanted in a man. Perhaps I would have been able to notice the very bright and very large red flags that appeared in the beginning of our relationship.

Shortly after we began dating, the fighting started. I had never met anyone with whom I disagreed so much. If I said white, he said black. We could never agree on anything. I felt as if he were trying to pull me away from my friends. It was as if he were jealous of any relationship I had that didn't include him. I began to doubt my ability to make smart decisions. The result was the slow annihilation of whatever self-esteem remained after being dumped by Mr. Wonderful.

Slowly, I began to change to please him. My friends disappeared and were replaced by his friends, school took a backseat and I had no hobbies or activities that didn't include him. My obsession with pleasing him was my only focus in life. I kept thinking that if I could just change certain aspects of my personality and stop certain behaviors, that he would finally be happy and we would finally have the kind of relationship that I knew we could have. To my surprise, the fights still continued after I made all of those changes trying to please him. No matter what I did, it was never right. It was a vicious circle. My ex-husband began affirming everything I had felt about myself. I felt just as unworthy, selfish, stupid and ugly as I did before Mr. Wonderful came into my life.

The loss of my own identity became worse with each passing year. My first priority was our relationship. The decisions I made at the time were not based on what was best for me, but what was best for "us." Your 20s are supposed to be a time that you use to explore life and discover who you are, what you stand for and how you want to live. My 20s were spent trying to please someone else.

By year four of our relationship, I was still struggling in school and was unsure of what I wanted to do with my life. I took dead-end jobs that did little to help me forge a career in a field that I loved. The only clear goal I had set for myself was to marry. My ex-husband began his career as a police officer during this time. Police academy training is relentless and tiring. Trying to be supportive, I began to take on "wifely" duties without getting that commitment from him. While he focused on training and studying, I focused on cooking his meals, cleaning his apartment, ironing his clothes and making sure his life was running as smooth as possible. Making myself indispensable to him would make him finally realize that I was a good person who deserved his respect and love.

Earning his respect and love was so important to my emotional and mental well being that I knew I couldn't rest or feel comfortable in our relationship until he proposed. One day in late July, he got down on one knee and asked me to be his wife. The sense of relief I felt after his proposal was enormous. It finally felt like I was going to be able to relax because we would be married soon and then he wouldn't leave me. Convinced that the fighting and criticisms would end, I accepted his proposal and began to fantasize about how perfect our life would be in the future. Looking back at this naiveté, I shudder with horror. But again, hindsight is 20/20.

The fighting didn't stop, if anything it worsened. Our fights had always been emotionally and verbally abusive but were now bordering on physical as well. Besides the usual rounds of name calling, on both our parts, I began to physically fear him. During one fight, he ripped all of my clothes out of our closet and threw them down the stairs. I was always the one to pursue the reconciliation. It wasn't long after the fight ended that I convinced myself that I was wrong and he was right. I believed that his anger was my fault. If I had only listened to him and changed my ways, he wouldn't get so angry.

Our wedding day came and passed and nothing significant changed in our relationship. Every one commented on how happy we looked on the day of our wedding. "You're the perfect couple," they would say. No one knew the extent of our problems because *I* didn't fully understand the extent of our problems. I had become so desperate to hang on to the relationship that I became desensitized to the horror of the fighting. This was my "normal."

Another two years passed and my care-taking behaviors continued. During this time, I graduated from college, but had yet to focus on my career. I only focused on his life. We bought a new house, which I set out to make the perfect home. To our friends and family, we seemed to have it all, but in reality the situation was becoming worse. The fighting continued and so did my desire to change myself to make him happy. I even resorted to making lists of all the things that I could change in order to calm the troubled waters at home. We moved closer to his family and further away from mine, which made the feeling of isolation worse.

Being married to a police officer is difficult even when the relationship is healthy. They have demanding schedules and often witness things at work that civilians could only imagine. They forge an incredible bond with their colleagues, which, in my case, led to many nights alone. He only wanted to be with his fellow officers. We saw each other only two weeks of the month because of his schedule and when he was home it was tense. The rigors of his job had taken a toll on his mental health causing him to be withdrawn and distant. When my husband was accepted into the police academy, the older officers sat down with family members and told them of the changes their loved ones would go through. I was witnessing these changes firsthand and was sure that it was all just a phase. One woman, whose husband was also on the force, told me that her husband went through a similar stage and quickly returned to normal. I waited patiently for my husband to pass through this phase and return to his normal self. He never did.

If anything, he was getting more brazen in his behavior. He had a four-day weekend and decided that he wanted to go camping with some friends instead of staying with me. He went to a friend's wedding alone and, claiming he had too much to drink, stayed in a hotel for the night. He played golf on his days off and if he was home, he'd spend time in the backyard talking to our neighbor. It felt like he would do anything to avoid being home and being alone with me.

As I adjusted to these changes, I began enjoying my time alone; savoring the peace and contentment I had when my husband wasn't home. But, when he was, I walked around my house on eggshells for fear that one wrong move would set him off. When we did fight, it was usually about money. Even though I was working full-time and earning only a few thousand dollars less than him, he convinced me that I was stupid and that he was supporting me. I became so guilt ridden over this I left a job I marginally enjoyed for one where I made a little more money, but hated with a passion.

The first two years of our marriage were difficult for so many reasons. We struggled with money issues, buying a brand new house, moving, and the loss of my beloved grandmother, which took a huge toll on my emotional health. My husband couldn't deal with me when I was upset. He wanted me to grieve on his schedule and when I didn't follow his plan, he resorted to his old habits again. He left the house without telling me where he was going, he never wanted to go out with me and when he was home we never talked, let alone touched. When we were alone together, we sat in silence. It was as if a large elephant was in the corner of the room and we were both denying its existence. The elephant was his misery; his absolute desire to leave me.

Completely emotionally drained, I had begun to isolate myself from my family. It was too difficult to hide the pain I was in and I didn't want them to interfere or to tell me what I knew in my heart –that my marriage was headed for disaster. Struggling to remain optimistic, I let my husband get away with his loathsome behavior because I was desperate to hang on to what I knew as "normal."

The last four months of my marriage were among the worst months of my life. After a terrible fight one August, he walked out after telling me he wanted a divorce. I waited for him to come home and when he did, I begged him to stay. In September, we made plans to go out one night after he got off work. After five hours of waiting and endless calls to his cell phone, I left in search of him convinced that he was in a car accident and dead. I was on the verge of a nervous breakdown when he called and told me he had gone out with people from work. That moment was horrible for me as the realization of what my marriage had become started to sink in. I can't recall feeling worse about my life as I did at that moment.

October and November brought more of the same. Our second anniversary came around and he never bothered to get me a card or a present. He was never home and I began to feel myself wondering what it would be like to be with someone else. I was desperate for affection and love and thought about cheating, but I was so diminished as a person that I thought no one would want me. I'm ashamed that I contemplated cheating on him, but I'm more ashamed that I convinced myself that I would never be able to find someone else to love me. Despite my thoughts of infidelity, I never would have cheated on my husband. I believed in my wedding vows and prided myself on being a good wife. My whole identity had revolved around being his wife and I couldn't contemplate not fulfilling that role.

The fear of being by myself and leaving the comfort and security of the relationship, even though it was destructive, stopped me from making changes in my life. I went through the motions every day, but I was sinking further into a depression that I was afraid would kill me. I honestly believe I would have stayed in this pattern forever, if fate hadn't intervened on the morning of December 5th.

It was a Thursday morning and an early snowstorm made travel from my small town into the city difficult. My husband had off, but working for a demanding boss left me fearful of calling in due to bad weather. Venturing out into the snow, I only made it halfway to work before I was forced to turn around. I called home and told my husband that I was coming back and he told me that he picked up a side job working as mall security. When I entered the house after making it carefully home in one piece, I heard my husband in the shower. The phone rang, I answered it and the line went dead. After checking the caller ID, I recognized the number from my husband's cell phone bill. The number began appearing so frequently in June that I asked my husband who it belonged to. He assured me that it was a male friend from work. Knowing the friend myself, I decided to call the number to make sure everything was okay. That's when it happened. I got *her* voice mail. I kept calling over and over again until she picked up. I asked, "Who is this?" and she hung up again.

I knew in my heart what was happening. Heading up the stairs to the master bathroom, I faced my husband as he was getting out of the shower. Handing him the phone, I said, "She called." For a moment, we both stared at each other in pained silence.

"I don't think I want to know who she is and why she keeps calling you," I said as I left the bathroom. Then, I went downstairs to the kitchen unsure of what to do or say. I was shutting down. The next few moments were a blur as he followed me downstairs. I remember him telling me her name and telling me that it wasn't what I thought. It felt like being punched in the stomach.

He denied, from the very beginning, that they were having a sexual relationship, but rather an emotional affair. He accused me of being sick and twisted to believe that he would cheat on me. He became increasingly angry and within moments exploded. He began screaming that our marriage was over and that I was a piece of trash he had wasted the last eight years of his life with. And then he left. He left me slumped on the kitchen floor. He left me for another woman.

When I turned from the front door that morning and looked around my house, I was unaware of the journey that lay ahead of me. I existed on a moment-to-moment basis. Any thought or action that required premeditation was too complex. My first night alone was one of the hardest for me. Unable to sleep, I spent the night sitting in my bed staring out the window waiting for him to come home. He never did.

The next day at work I was indescribably jovial. In my mind it was a terrible mistake and would be rectified as soon as I could talk to him. The extent of his deception wasn't fully realized at that moment. I didn't understand that his moodiness and his absence from my life were because he was so unhappy in the marriage. I still assumed his job pressures were causing him to act out like he had been. His mother, with whom I had a turbulent relationship, convinced me to come over to her house and talk about the situation. No one in his family had heard from him and panic began to set in. As I sat in my mother-in-law's kitchen, I replayed the whole scenario for her. My husband called his parents' house later that evening and he agreed to talk to me the next night.

Knowing that I'd see him in less than 24 hours, I felt so incredibly happy. It seemed like I was on the path to putting my marriage back together. As we sat on the couch, I remember thinking that we would have this talk, go upstairs to our bedroom and then go to sleep. Convinced that when we woke up in the morning, everything would be back to normal and I could continue living this comfortable, yet completely unfulfilling life that I had been living for so many years. It was all I yearned for. I needed nothing else, but to have things go back to the way they were no matter how horrible they were. Change was not my friend. The fear of being alone outweighed the fear of being in a bad marriage.

The night did not go how I had envisioned and it ended in an argument. Upset, I asked him if he was having a sexual relationship with her and he said no. They had met a few months earlier while she was working for the police department. I forced myself to believe every word he told me that night. I believed it because I thought he would come home. But when I asked him to come home and work on the marriage, he told me that he couldn't. He said he needed time and that he wished no one in our families knew what had happened between us. Feeling furious that he wouldn't stay with me, I yelled at him. He yelled back before storming out of the house.

It was obvious to everyone but me at the time that I was in denial. People told me that going through a divorce was like grieving a death. The same five stages apply. The first stage, denial, lasted a long time. I was in pure denial for at least six weeks, waiting every night for him to come home. I constantly called him and I even offered to pick up his dry cleaning once. To think back and realize that I was running his errands after finding out he was having an affair with another woman makes me physically ill. He occasionally came home and stayed in the guest room. We were only rooms away from each other, but it felt like miles.

We talked on a regular basis and I kept asking him if he was ready to come home to me, but he kept saying he needed more time. This pattern lasted for about six weeks. Then one day in January, he called and mentioned that he was thinking about coming home. I was ecstatic. This was the moment I was waiting for and we made plans to meet one night to discuss our relationship. Before this meeting could happen, he called me at work and told me that our marriage was over. He said he couldn't get past the fact that my family knew what had happened and he could never face them again. At that moment, I moved into stage two of the grieving process – anger.

The day after my husband announced that our marriage was over, I launched into "get even" mode. After collecting and examining every phone bill, the picture of his betrayal and deception became clearer. He had met her in June or July, six months before I knew of her existence. Sometimes he would call her 20 times a day. There were phone calls after I went to bed at night and after I went to work in the morning. He called her while he was working and she called him too. There were times that he was on the phone with me and when she called, he would put me on hold to talk to her. The only time her number was missing was the four-day camping trip he took with his "friends." The cell phone bills I received and paid after he left me showed the same pattern. On the day he told me that he was considering coming home, he called her at least 10 times. This realization fueled a fire in me. I contacted a divorce attorney and made plans to file a separation agreement.

When I met with the attorney, he could sense that I was out for blood and suggested that we take an easier approach to the divorce that would leave me better off financially. I'm so grateful for the wisdom of that attorney who helped me. A long, drawn-out divorce in a no-fault state would have been a painful process and would not have helped me heal. Instead, he drew up a separation agreement and I delivered it to my husband on February 5th.

My husband was living with his parents at the time and I remember the triumphant feeling I had walking into their house to deliver the separation agreement. Unfortunately, the high didn't last long. When I got into my car to drive back to "my house," the anger stage disappeared as quickly as it came and I was left with the most unattractive of all the stages – bargaining.

For me, this was the worst stage because it was the time in my life when I was at my lowest. I had no self-esteem and second guessed every aspect of my marriage. There were days at work where I sat in my boss' office on the phone with my mother replaying every moment of my marriage in my head. I kept saying to her, "If only I had done..." It didn't matter what the end of the sentence was. If I would have just done everything differently, maybe I wouldn't have driven him to cheat. I even tried to bargain with God. I could have written a book called, "Dear God, It's me Michelle." My prayers would be variations of, "Dear Lord, if you bring him home to me, I will go to church every Sunday and never say another curse word."

The bargaining never worked, which led me straight to the next stage – depression. The depression I'd been in since he left worsened. I cried more and believed my families' words of encouragement less. Isolating myself, I wanted little to do with my friends who were still happily married and I found myself living like a hermit. My days consisted of getting up in the morning, taking a shower, going to work, driving home and getting back into bed. Guilty feelings filled my head and I began to blame myself for the end of my marriage. Unable to eat, I eventually lost 25 pounds.

The depression also stemmed from what I believed to be my fate. The self-esteem that I had lacked before my marriage was now worse than ever. Thoughts of being alone for the rest of my life plagued me during this time. I knew from an early age that I always wanted children and my husband and I had been trying to get pregnant. Now, not only was I getting divorced at the age of 28, but my plans for motherhood were on hold indefinitely. I thought I was never going to find someone and have the family I so much desired. This thought crippled me, sending me further into a depression as I was slowly facing the reality that I might never get the opportunity to be a mother.

It was during this depression that I realized that he was not coming home and our marriage was over. I had reached the last stage of the grieving process – acceptance. The acceptance stage does not come with a guarantee of happiness. It was not as if I woke up one morning and said to myself, "Hey, I accept that my marriage is over. Let's party!" You don't immediately wake up happy and healed. You literally just realize that what you've been fighting so desperately to hold onto is gone and that everything you believe to be true is false. My marriage was not going to be saved.

Most days I would sit in silence. My house was empty and my heart felt the same way. At the time, the silence was deafening. I couldn't stand being alone and felt lonely and afraid. Insomnia was my partner most nights. As soon as my head touched the pillow, my brain went into overdrive. During the day, it's amazing how much of your time can be filled with meaningless chores. The night was a different story. There was little to distract me from the thoughts of divorce that swirled through my head. I came to embrace the insomnia and learned a little about myself along the way. I'm very fortunate to live in a town where people feel safe enough that they don't lock their doors. This allowed me to leave my house at midnight and take a walk without fear of being attacked.

These midnight walks eased my mind. With headphones on, I would listen to Norah Jones as I walked down the street in my pajamas. One night in February, it began to snow on my walk. I remember the smell of the snow before it made its presence known. I remember the way it looked as it fell from the sky and the coldness as it landed on my face. It was the first time that I ever existed in the moment. I remember every detail of that walk. I had never in my life just existed. Like most people, I'm always thinking about chores that need to be done or bills I have to pay. Many of us never take a minute to appreciate our surroundings. I learned from those walks how to live in the moment.

With some self-examination and the help of a therapist, two things occurred to me at this point. First, I was back at square one. It was literally as if I was looking at myself the day before Mr. Wonderful came into my life. Only, eight years had passed. I still had no clue what made me happy and no clue how to look at my mistakes and take lessons from them. I felt unworthy of love, ugly and stupid.

Second, I realized that my unhappiness was not stemming from the loss of my husband, but rather the loss of the life I wanted so badly. I didn't miss him. He was a jerk and at the end of the marriage I preferred to be alone, but I missed the idea of him. I was mourning the security of being married and the idea that motherhood was only a few years away.

The realization of these ideas marked a turning point in my life. I knew what I had to do. First and foremost, I had to determine what made me happy without a relationship. I could no longer depend on a man for my happiness. Second, I knew that I had to create a life for myself where fear of being alone didn't outweigh the fear of being in a destructive relationship. I wish that I could say that from that moment on I was happy and confident. Nothing could be further from the truth. That "AHA" moment marked the beginning of a roller coaster ride of emotions for me. It was not easy, but at that moment, I chose myself. For the first time in my life, I chose my life over a man. That's the moment the real work began.

During the first four stages of the grieving process, I was still trying to lead a normal life. I had bills, which meant I had to work and I had to maintain a household as well. Going through the motions of my daily life I hadn't been giving any real thought to what I was doing. It wasn't until I made the decision to discover myself that I realized, even though my husband was gone, I was still living my life as if he were there. I was behaving as if he were going to walk in the house at any moment. My first trip to the grocery store, post AHA moment, was one I will never forget. Absentmindedly, I picked up the usual items until it occurred to me that I was buying the groceries he liked. In the eight years we were together I never once thought about what food I would like to eat. I spent nearly two hours going down the aisles picking foods that I knew my husband didn't like. By the time I got to the checkout I had a cart full of food that I had never tried and wasn't sure if I was going to like. It was moments like this that helped me to discover myself. Something as simple as deciding that I didn't like red velvet cake, but adored pineapple upside down cake gave me a confidence that I hadn't felt in years. I knew something about myself that I hadn't known before. I started with the small stuff before I tackled the big questions in my life. I could wait to figure out what I wanted out of a relationship. At that moment, I needed to know if I liked penne or ziti pasta better.

I found out that I loved sleeping in very expensive pajamas from Victoria's Secret while lying in the middle of my bed. I loved waking up on a Sunday morning, gathering all of my new books that I acquired from my new favorite activity, browsing the bookstore, and lying in bed while eating scrambled eggs and cheese. I loved dancing in my underwear to the Bee Gees. These new discoveries made me realize that I had known some things about myself, but had forgotten them because I was wrapped up in someone else's happiness. I've always loved reading mysteries and watching old movies in black and white. I had simply forgotten.

Even though I was having fun and discovering myself all over again, each day was not a ball of sunshine. There were many days where I went through all five stages of grief in one sitting. I would believe that our marriage was still fixable, get angry with him for cheating, beg God to bring him home if I went to church, eat an entire pineapple upside down cake when I was depressed and then realize that the marriage was over.

Not all people go through the stages at the same rate or in the same order. I believed in one moment that I was healed and completely over him and then would find myself locked in the bathroom at work because a song came on the radio that we danced to at our wedding. The process is long and painful and sometimes lasts for years.

Three years later, I still get a slight punch in the stomach when someone mentions his name. There were two days in particular that were really bad though. The day my husband filed for divorce and the day the divorce decree became final. After enough time passed, I learned to live my life without thinking much of the divorce process and then all of a sudden I was thrown back in the middle of the drama. Those days were bad, but they passed rather quickly.

Every emotion I felt at the time was important. I learned the hard way to feel what I was feeling at the moment rather than push the emotion aside. It was important for me to understand the feelings I was having so I could move forward. Otherwise, the emotion keeps surfacing without being resolved. That's the only way to truly heal. For me, each day became better. I would cry a little less or not at all.

I sought refuge in my friendships. It was very difficult for me to talk to my married girlfriends about my divorce because they couldn't understand the absolute pain of it. They couldn't understand why I felt like a failure. If not for a group of women I found on the Internet, I would not have found the strength some days to keep going. It was a group of women who were all going through a divorce under the age of 30. These women became my sisters, my friends, my confidantes and I've never met them face-to-face. I never needed to. Their words provided enormous comfort to me at my worst. Seeking comfort from people who understood what I was dealing with saved not only me, but saved my family from having to listen over and over to the sad stories I was telling. These women were my lifesavers most days.

They were also my therapists, even when I wasn't seeking advice; for instance, when I got involved with a man only three months after my husband left. They all cautioned me against dating someone too soon and too seriously. My neighbor, whom had been friendly with my ex-husband, knew we were separated and came over to offer help around the house if I needed it. At the time, I didn't think of him romantically. Our dogs were friends and would spend hours chasing each other through the neighborhood. We became friends too.

It wasn't long after we started spending time together that our friendship turned into more. I blame it on the margaritas, but in reality I knew what I wanted. I wasn't looking for a boyfriend or a new husband. I was looking for physical affection that made me feel good. My friends told me this was a "friends with benefits" relationship and they helped guide me through the tough terrain of keeping my feelings at a distance, but still enjoying the "benefits."

This was the perfect arrangement for me. I was having my physical needs met without having to commit to anyone. In my head, we weren't dating; therefore, there were no attachments. Holding onto the space I needed to explore my new freedom, I discovered myself. For the most part, I could disassociate my feelings for my friend with the physical part of our relationship because I was starved for the physical contact that had been missing during my marriage. However, every now and then panic would set in and I would distance myself from my "friend."

I was afraid we were getting too serious about each other and I didn't want to lose myself in another relationship. This fear kept me from realizing my true feelings for many months, but it also helped me to remember that my main goal in life was to learn about myself independent of a relationship.

One day I remember getting ready for work and looking at my reflection in the mirror. Smiling at myself for the first time in my life, I realized I was happy with what I saw reflected back, both physically and mentally. I had become comfortable in my own skin. My first thought was that I had finally made all of those changes that I was desperate to make while I was married. Then I realized that I really hadn't changed. My true self had finally been given the opportunity to come out without fear of rejection. I was no longer living my life to please someone else, but living to please me. It was the first time in my whole adult life that I felt like a woman.

A few months later I finally admitted to my friends, even though they already knew, and to myself that I was in love with my "friend." I wasn't as good at having a "friends with benefits" relationship as I thought. Our relationship had grown and I realized that he was a caring, compassionate man with whom I had a lot in common. I got very lucky. During my time of retrospection and discovery I never took the time to decide what I wanted out of a relationship. I was too busy discovering what made me happy.

Through the process of self-discovery, I gained the confidence that I needed to recognize what I wouldn't tolerate in a relationship. I knew that I never would tolerate lying or cheating. Luckily for me, my "friend" never displayed any behavior that would have warranted a red flag alert in my head. Though if he had, I know that I would have been strong enough to walk away. I was not the same person I was in my marriage. I knew that I wouldn't trade what I wanted most for what I wanted in the moment.

When I finally admitted we were dating, our relationship changed. Now my feelings were on the line and soon all my insecurities came back into the picture. These insecurities were not the same ones that plagued me during my first two serious relationships. I no longer felt unworthy of love, stupid or ugly, but rather became overly concerned that he was going to cheat on me. A new crop of insecurities had harvested because of the divorce. My boyfriend never gave me any reason to think he was cheating. He behaved in a completely different way than my husband. He understood what the divorce had done to me. He was patient and understanding and allowed me to have my insecurities without making me feel badly about being suspicious. He would often just look at me and say, "I'm not him." Eventually the insecurities became less prevalent and I allowed myself to trust again. It was difficult, but in the end it was worth it. I knew that I was no longer letting the fear of getting hurt ruin my chance of happiness. Finding the confidence in me to make the choices I knew were right for me was empowering.

Almost three years later, I look back on the time I struggled through the divorce with great pride. During the first days after my ex-husband left, I begged and pleaded with God to give me my old life back. Now, I wouldn't go back to the way I was living for anything in the world. The divorce was the most painful time in my life, yet one of the most profound. I'm no longer the girl I was before, but a woman who knows that she can get through any challenge. I developed friendships with women that will last a lifetime.

I've developed a friendship with myself that will never leave me lonely. My life is a priority. My happiness is a priority.

Now as I write this story, I'm listening to my daughter play with my husband. My "friend" and I were married last year. I spent no time planning it and I remember every last detail of the vows we exchanged. We have a daughter. She is the light of my life. If I hadn't been through that pain, if I hadn't struggled with my self-esteem and identity issues, I never would have met this man who accepts me for me. I never would have my daughter. I still have the same values I had when I was married to my ex-husband. I still pride myself on being a good wife, but this time it's different. I have the self-esteem to demand respect and honesty from my partner. I have someone to love and who, in return, loves me without judgment.

No one wants to get divorced, yet it happens. And when it happens you need to take the lessons you learn and create the life you want. Life does not have to end after divorce. For most of us, it's a chance to start over and to experience life with a wisdom we would not have gained if we were still married.

When she's older I will tell my daughter this story without shame. I used to wear the shame of being "divorced" like a scarlet D on my chest. I'm smarter, wiser, funnier, stronger, happier and healthier because of my divorce. She may not take to heart the lessons I will try to teach her from my experience. She may repeat my mistakes and that will be all right. She will learn the lessons the hard way, but at least they will have been learned.

Her laughter rings through my home and it brings me back to the moment when I turned from the front door and stared at my empty and silent house. In that silence, I learned about life and love. I learned that silence can be deafening, but sometimes necessary to help you find what you are looking for. As I navigated through the silent rooms of my old house, I found my real home. It doesn't have walls or windows. There are no appliances or even a bed. My home exists within me. It's the place I go to everyday. The place within me that guides me through difficult times and helps me determine the next path I will take in my life. It's the place where I learned to listen to my gut, stop taking my cues from others and finally found the peace of mind for which I had been searching. I learned, because of the divorce, that my home is my true self. My home is me.

How to Become Young, Divorced and Fabulous!

As we went through our divorces, we often asked ourselves, what the hell am I going to do? We felt like we failed so early in our lives and our chance at happily ever after was gone. Gone, kaput, vaporized. We wondered if we'd be able to pick up the pieces of our lives and go on. It seemed like such a daunting task but we were up for the challenge. It's been a few years since we wrote our divorce memoirs. Since then, we've embraced our second chances and created lives we couldn't even imagine when we were going through our divorces. Between the four of us, we've celebrated two new marriages, the birth of seven children and welcomed the addition of three new pets. Life *does* go on after a divorce and it can go on to be something amazing. All of us are happier than we ever thought possible. In this final chapter, we're going to fill you in on what's happened in the past few years since our divorces and we're going to share with you our sisterly advice on the two best ways we've found to kick start being young, divorced and fabulous!

Sisterly Advice #1 – You have to Grieve!

"I remember lying on the floor of my bathtub sobbing hysterically when I realized my marriage was over. The pain I felt that day and for many days that followed was an intense, crushing, suffocating feeling that made me wonder how it didn't kill me. But, it didn't and I began to wonder if there was something to that saying, 'what doesn't kill you, makes you stronger.' It took me several months to start feeling better and then slowly the good days started to outnumber the bad," recalls Karen Jerabek.

Healing from a divorce is actually a grieving process. It's common to grieve for the marriage that's lost, for the best friend that's gone, the future that isn't going to happen and the children that aren't going to be born. Having a short marriage does not diminish the difficulty and stress that a divorce causes. It's an extremely painful experience. Besides the death of a spouse, the next most stressful event in someone's life is a divorce. Dr. Kubler-Ross, renowned psychiatrist, researched grief and highlighted five critical stages. Healing from a divorce involves these same stages of grief.

Stages of Divorce Grief

Stage 1: Denial – This is the initial "Leave it to Beaver" stage when you don't want to accept that your marriage is over and you pretend that the divorce isn't going to happen. You slap a smile on your face and go about your business acting like your marriage and your life are just fine because you don't want to face the writing on the wall. This may occur before the "divorce talk" when you feel like your marriage isn't working out or it may happen when your spouse tells you he wants a divorce. Either way, it's common to react by thinking, "this isn't happening."

Stage 2: Anger – This is the "Raging Bull" stage when you really get pissed off at your spouse and at the situation. It's common to yell and scream and throw things. It can be difficult to keep these emotions under control. It's important to find a positive outlet, whether you go to the gym or vent to your girlfriends. Part of the anger stage is turning the anger inward which results in feelings of guilt. You feel guilty about what you did, what you didn't do and what your family is going to think when they find out about your divorce. Guilt can eat away at you and is especially strong among women. If you feel overwhelmed by emotions of anger, you may act out in ways that could lead to dangerous choices and possible legal action.

Stage 3: Bargaining – In the "Victoria's Secret" stage, the initial anger has worn off and you want to go back to how things were when they were good. You want to fix your marriage or yourself so that you can avoid getting divorced. You may try going to couples counseling. Or, you may tell yourself that if you only lost 5lbs or bought some new sexy lingerie, he'd find you attractive again and you'd be able to rekindle the passion in your marriage. Regardless of your attempts to reconcile your relationship, things don't improve which leads you into the next stage.

Stage 4: Depression – This "Ugly Cry" stage is when the sadness and the tears and the Kleenex are overflowing. You find yourself wanting to stay in bed all day and you don't want to leave the house or go to work. It's hard to find motivation to do anything except cry.

Stage 5: Acceptance – This is the final "Letting Go" stage. You've accepted your divorce and made peace with it. It doesn't mean that you're happy about it but it doesn't define you anymore. You don't talk about it incessantly, you don't think about what he's doing every day and most days you don't even think about the fact that you're divorced.

The grieving process isn't a straight line to healing. You don't go down the list, checking each one off. Typically, you cycle through the stages and bounce between them before settling into acceptance. Even once you've made your way into the acceptance stage it's not unusual to have something as simple as a song on the radio trigger strong emotions. Usually the trigger comes out of the blue and catches you off guard. If you're truly in the acceptance stage, the feeling is brief and you go back to living your life. If you aren't fully in the acceptance stage, then this event can cause a break down and pull you back into one of the other stages to continue healing. You can't rush the healing process and there is no specific time line. It's important to be kind to yourself as you navigate through your feelings.

All of us worked through our emotions in our own ways and struggled with different stages, but, in the end, we made it through and emerged as strong young women. We often get asked what helped us get through the grief of our divorces. Here are the key steps we used that helped us reach the acceptance stage.

Key Steps to Reaching Acceptance

1. Honor the grief experience. The most important thing you can do through your divorce is to feel the emotions that you have, acknowledge and accept them and then seek out the good that is coming from this experience. Karen Jerabek wasn't comfortable with her feelings of anger so she suppressed them. It was two years later, when she couldn't push them down any longer that they finally emerged, demanding that she finally pay attention to them. Trying to ignore your feelings only lasts for so long. Eventually they will come up and you will have to deal with them. The sooner you face them, the sooner you can move forward toward healing. As you move toward healing, you'll eventually be able to say, I'm really glad I'm divorced and you'll be able to list off a bunch of reasons why that's true. It probably seems impossible now, but one day, you'll realize you made it through the tunnel and you'll be standing on the other side, stronger than ever.

2. Create a support network. It's important to find people that can really understand what you're going through. In order to get that understanding, you need to seek out people who are also going through a divorce. The four of us stumbled upon a message board while we were looking for divorce recovery resources and it provided us a space to vent and share our feelings. We also had the opportunity to give and receive support with other women that were going through the same thing. Our friendships developed on that message board and now we're best friends both online and off. It was a huge relief for all of us to have that support and we each know that our lives wouldn't be the same if we hadn't found each other. Even though that message board isn't around anymore, there are divorce support groups online, divorce recovery programs through local churches such as Divorce Care and in your community, like divorce groups on meetup.com. Individually, we each sought out therapy as well. Having a professional validate your feelings and help you navigate this new phase of your life can be very useful. We encourage you to explore the different opportunities that are out there and then find the ones that are a good fit for you so you can continue to have the support that you need as you go through this challenging time.

3. Let your family and friends be there for you. Seek out the supportive family members and friends that are in your life and open up to them about what you're going through. Not all of them are going to be supportive, and those that are will be able to offer different types of support. You'll need to figure out what kind of support you need and then see who in your life can offer that to you. Allow them to comfort you and help you pick up the pieces so that moving on can be a little easier. Michelle Nicolet did this by moving home to live with her mom so that she could afford to finish her Master's Program. Once at home, she had the love and support of her family and was able to continue her education while healing from her divorce. It was a tough transition going from being married and owning her own house, to moving home with her mom but she was able to continue her educational dreams by making that choice and she was able to have her mom's daily support and friendship.

4. Have faith. When grief strikes, it's common to look for answers within the context of your religious and spiritual beliefs. You may be tempted to turn your back on your faith because you feel like this shouldn't be happening to you. Michelle Denicola Poole chose to look for answers within her religious convictions. She looked to scripture and talked with various people within her church to find acceptance and understanding.

5. Rediscover yourself. You've been so focused on your marriage and your partner that you've probably neglected yourself. It's important to take time to get to know yourself again. After years of focusing on her husband, Michelle Joyce wasn't even sure what food she liked. She had always bought the food her husband preferred. After they separated, she took delight in trying all kinds of new dishes! This really is the best time to try some of the things you'd always wanted to try, but kept putting off.

6. Share your love. Finding an opportunity to reconnect to your loving nature helps bring joy and hope into your life again. Many of us have pets and found comfort in the unconditional love that they offered us. Karen Jerabek's love for her two dogs helped ease the ache in her heart. Her dogs brought her happiness and she enjoyed taking them on hikes in the woods or just cuddling on the couch. She found that her apartment was filled with love even though there was a person missing from their family. Whether you have pets or not, this is also a great time for you to volunteer and help someone in need. Divorce can leave you feeling like a failure, but when you help someone else you start to recognize your value and you feel good about making a difference. Whether your passion is for animals, children or helping the homeless, you can find an opportunity to help others by choosing to participate in a volunteer program or do volunteer work on your own, like offering to babysit your neighbor's kids for the afternoon, taking your dog for a special walk, calling a friend who's also having a rough time or bringing a sandwich to the homeless person that you drive by every day. When we give to someone else, we're also giving to ourselves.

7. Practice gratitude. Finding things in our daily life to be thankful for allows us to step outside of our grief and appreciate the good that is going on around us all the time. On our message board, we would do a Thankful Thursday post where each of us would post three things. As you start thinking about what you're grateful for, be specific and focus on what happened in the past few days, like being grateful that your best friend came by for coffee or that a meeting with your boss went well. You can download a gratitude app on your phone with a reminder set up so that each day you can add three things that happened during the day that you're grateful for, both big and small. This also provides an opportunity to focus on the positives in life so instead of saying that you're grateful you aren't sick, it's more impactful to say that you're thankful that you're healthy and strong. So, flip around any negatives and you'll be on your way to positive living.

After getting to this point in the book, you should be realizing that your feelings are totally normal and that everyone going through a divorce feels just like you. You aren't alone. Hallelujah, because feeling alone while you're going through such a devastating loss sucks. Maybe you don't feel great, but we bet you're starting to feel a little better. We've shared with you the stages of grief and we've given you the keys to reaching acceptance so that you can finally feel free. The more you allow yourself to grieve, the more you'll be ready for the transformative power of our second dose of sisterly advice.

Sisterly Advice #2 – Embrace Joy

Up until now, your entire focus has been on getting through your divorce. You were in survival mode just trying to take it day by day. But now that you've survived the divorce and can actually catch your breath, it's time to start looking towards the future and what's just around the corner in your new life. It's time to stand up and proudly claim your right to be young, divorced and fabulous!

The second thing you need to do in order to become young, divorced and fabulous is to embrace joy! That may seem laughable right now, especially if you've just come out of one hell of a divorce, but that's okay. Divorce tends to suck all of the joy out of life which is why it's so important to not only find joy again, but to embrace it wholeheartedly and with wild enthusiasm. And, don't worry - it's surprisingly easy to do.

Anything, absolutely anything that makes you laugh or brings a smile to your face adds joy to your life. That is what you want to seek more of right now. On the flip side, anything that makes you sad or makes you cry, you want to avoid like the plague. No more tear-jerking books or depressing movies even if they are winning Oscars. Your goal right now is to seek pleasure, period.

Make a quick list of things that bring you joy. Seriously, write it down. Do flowers make you happy? Then pick up a bouquet next time you're at the grocery store. Do you laugh at reruns of the Simpsons? Then indulge in an afternoon of watching them next weekend. And, don't worry if your list seems short because it's actually quite normal after a crisis to be disconnected from your feelings of joy. Use your list as a starting point for you to begin focusing on your joy again. This is also an opportunity to start looking for new things to try. Sign up for that class you've thought about taking. Go out with your co-workers after work one evening. Start saying yes to invites and giving these opportunities a chance to bring joy into your life. You'll be surprised how quickly your life starts to overflow with joy once you start making it a point to do the things that bring you laughter and put a smile on your face. Once you embrace joy, you'll find that you really are *young, divorced and fabulous!*

Happily Divorced

The four of us married in our twenties, had short lived marriages and were divorced by the time we hit 30. As we climbed out of the wreckage of our failed marriages, we found ourselves with an amazing opportunity for reinvention. We had molded ourselves to fit our marriages and now that those marriages were broken, we were free to be whoever we wanted to be. The hardest part was letting go of the path we'd been on. Divorce brings you to your knees, stripping everything away; all of your hopes and dreams and it leaves you completely vulnerable. You find yourself back at square one. This new found vulnerability also brings freedom. This was a scary idea at first, but the more we thought about it, the more exciting it became. We soon discovered that we could go down any number of new roads that were laid out right in front of us. It's been a few years since we wrote our memoirs and we've each taken different paths and had different journeys. We've learned that life isn't perfect, there is no happily ever after, but there *is* such a thing as being happily divorced.

Karen Jerabek

When I left my husband, I spent six months cocooned in a single bedroom apartment. After spending some time licking my wounds, I decided to buy my very first house. I found a cute townhouse with a neighborhood pool where you could watch the sun set over a state park. As soon as I drove into the neighborhood, I knew this was it. I didn't even look at houses in any other area. I bought a "for sale by owner" and was proud of myself for negotiating an awesome deal. As I was moving in, I met and soon started dating one of my neighbors. After enjoying my solitude, I felt ready to start being social again. We walked the dogs together, hung out at the pool together, cooked together and eventually worked together when he got me a job in real estate. We had fun, but it wasn't going anywhere. The thought of yet another relationship not working out terrified me. I pushed to make it work and he withdrew. After we'd been together a year, he still didn't want a commitment so I ended the relationship. He lived four doors down from me and it was excruciating to watch different girls pull up to his house night after night. As I felt the pain of this break up, I finally started to feel the pain of my divorce too. I was overwhelmed with grief and anger and sadness.

A friend of mine asked me to fly out to California to visit her so that I could get away from the situation. I booked a flight and left a few days later. It was exactly what I needed. I cleared my head, enjoyed spending time with my friend and had some fun in Los Angeles. I came back feeling a little saner than when I left. I still felt distraught at times, so I booked an appointment with a therapist. I was sweating and overcome with anxiety as I left a message asking for an appointment. I hated feeling like my emotions were out of my control. I hadn't been to therapy while I was married or when my marriage ended and I didn't realize how much I needed to talk about my divorce until this relationship fell apart. I spent a year going to therapy every week and it was such an eye opening, comforting experience. My only regret is that I didn't go sooner.

While I continued to wade back into the dating pool, I reconnected with a college friend. I had been searching for him on and off through the years and then one night, I stumbled upon an email address for him. He called me as soon as he got my email and it was like time had stood still. We were laughing and joking like we'd seen each other yesterday. He wanted to see me, but we were now living on opposite sides of the country. I booked a flight and three weeks later, I was in his arms. The sparks flew just as they had in college and it wasn't long before he told me he loved me. We had a connection that I had never experienced with anyone else. He understood me better than I understood myself and that hadn't changed, even after all these years. Being together was easy and it was fun and I was happy, really happy. It had always been that way between us. When it came time to say goodbye, it was more painful that I thought it would be. As soon as I got home, I booked another flight for a month later. That second trip was even more intense than the first. On my last night before flying home, he held my hand over a romantic dinner and talked about marrying me one day. Then two weeks later, he called me and said that he "couldn't do this anymore." He didn't want to talk about it, he didn't want to explain it, but he was very clear about one thing – we were over. I had just lost my job and now I was losing the man I loved, the man I had *always* loved. I felt like I was losing a part of myself, too.

He shut me out and when that phone call ended, I shut a door to my heart. How much heartache could one person endure anyways? I tried to forget him and I tried to move on, but the only thing I moved on to was a string of men that were sexy, exciting and younger than me. They were more diversions than anything else, kind of like a band-aid fix for my broken heart. I didn't want to trust anyone and I certainly didn't want to be vulnerable so I chose men who would be fun for a month or two, but nothing more. It seemed safer that way.

Even though post divorce dating was proving to be more troublesome than I had imagined, I was enjoying my life. I had a ton of friends and went out most nights. I played kickball in an adult league where we drank beer and played kickball for fun. I love listening to live music and would go out to hear bands and dance all night. I took a few trips with friends, heading to the mountains and the beach and going on a tubing adventure. I enjoyed taking my dogs to a local dog park and the state park for some exploring. I was having a great time!

Because I wasn't having much luck dating, I began to doubt that motherhood would come to me in the traditional way of falling in love and *then* having a child together. But, that was okay. I didn't need to be married in order to have a child. This is the 21st century after all. I was completely open to motherhood in any way it might enter my life - whether I adopted, fell in love with someone that had a child, or had one of my own. It sounds crazy, but I knew in my soul that I would be a mother and I would be celebrating Christmas two years from then with my baby, so I never worried about how that was going to happen or tried to plan it. I left it up to God and the Universe.

The following fall, I was surprised to find out that I was pregnant. I knew right from the beginning, that if I continued my pregnancy, I would be doing it alone as a single parent and that the biological father would not be part of our lives. I made the choice to become a single parent and, even though it was a scary choice, I was overjoyed to be embarking on my dream of motherhood.

153

My parents were shocked by the news, but quickly became excited at the idea of becoming grandparents. My mom wanted to be at every doctor's appointment and drove two hours every few weeks. My doctor's office does early ultrasounds and she was by my side during my first appointment excited to see her grandchild on the screen. We watched the ultrasound monitor marveling at my little baby that was growing inside of me. The doctor pointed at the screen and said, "Here's your baby." It looked like a tiny peanut in a large black sack. We watched the movements and I was about to cry when I noticed that the edge of the screen seemed to have another black section. At that moment, the doctor moved the ultrasound and exclaimed, "And here's your second baby!" My wish to be a mother was not only granted, it was doubled!

I sold my townhouse and moved home to live with my parents before the twins were born so I could have the support, love and help that I needed. Six and a half weeks early, I welcomed Kate and Lily into this world. Not only did I celebrate that Christmas with a baby, I celebrated with two!

The next few years that followed were a whirlwind. Raising twins was all consuming and I didn't have time for much else. When they were five months old, I went back to work full time and was overwhelmed by an intense workload and high expectations coupled with lack of sleep and very

154

little time with my babies. After several months, I transitioned into part time work that provided a better balance for me between my work and home life. In order to make that doable, I decided to continue living at my parent's house which has been great. My parents continue to be an amazing support for us and my mom watches the girls for me when I work. Sure, we can get on each other's nerves from time to time but I enjoy having Kate and Lily's grandparents in our lives every day. When they say it takes a village to raise a child, I definitely can see why.

After being single for a couple years, I slowly started dating again. This time, my outlook was completely different. I wanted a man that was going to make an amazing partner and father and I felt ready to start thinking about getting married again. Online dating sites seemed like a good way to get my feet wet and I've been able to meet some amazing men. The most recent one though, shook me to my core. When I saw him online, I was drawn to him. He emailed me, noting that we had traded emails a while back but had not met and he'd like the opportunity to get to know me. I recognized him but couldn't place the details and agreed. We had an amazing first date and the relationship that developed was easy and effortless. I was just happy, all the time. He went out of his way to do things for me and we saw each other several times a week. After dinner one night, we were sharing stories with each other about our lives and this was the first time I'd felt truly accepted and cared for by a man. While this is what I had been wanting so badly, the floodgates of my fear burst open. I started having flashbacks of painful relationship memories and I was having trouble sleeping. The more I tried to push them away, the faster they came and I felt like I couldn't close the doors as fast as they popped open. Overwhelmed and not really sure what was going on, I tried to steel myself and push through it. I found myself shoving the relationship forward while emotionally pulling back. I was scared and I didn't understand it. Panicking, I found myself acting critical and rejecting him. Our relationship ended in a matter of days.

While losing him was completely devastating for me, it was also the motivation I needed to finally take a closer look at how my fears were holding me back in life. I loved him so deeply that it caused all of this bottled up pain to come to the surface and I was determined to find a way to let it go. He's the only man that could have inspired this level of self reflection. I found an amazing life coach and started working with him to identify my patterns and the negative beliefs that I held in my subconscious so that I could release them and find a healthier way of being in a relationship. After a few months of intense work digging up the past and releasing it, I'm in a place of hope and peace. I'm starting to date someone new now and while it's moving at a slow, comfortable pace, we're connecting, it's fun and I have absolutely no idea where it might go. For the first time, I find this absolutely exhilarating. My focus is on enjoying the twists and turns and all the excitement that comes with it. One day, I'd like to get married again but I'm leaving that up to God and the Universe to figure out the details, just like I did with my desire to have a baby. In the meantime, I'm enjoying my two little girls, feeling content and happy with my life, just the way it is.

Michelle Nicolet

The year after my divorce, I focused on getting my life back on track. I busied myself with applying for jobs. I was unsuccessful, despite a couple of interviews and awesome references and grades. It was very frustrating. In retrospect though, I think it was a good thing. I was able to take a year off with minimal stress and just worry about putting one foot in front of the other. I wasn't ready for the stresses of a full time, first year teaching job. I needed time to heal first.

Six months later, I got an interview for an ideal teaching position. I had thrown myself into securing a job so thoroughly that I actually studied for interviews. I holed up in my room and read interview books, wrote out answers and practiced them. I knew I needed to move forward and a job symbolized that to me.

After the interview, I knew I nailed it. As I drove home, the song "A New Day Has Come" by Celine Dion came on the radio and I cried. Slowly, the tears turned into sobs as I consciously thought about releasing the past and allowing myself a new start. That song became important to me during that period and I'd listen to it again and again for inspiration and as a reminder that I could let go and move on. I found music to be very cathartic.

I landed the job and then quickly found myself an adorable condo to rent. My sister moved in with me, which was a comfort, as I wasn't really ready to go it alone yet. I had a real sense of hope. We excitedly picked out things for the house and that fall I started my job. I've been teaching for several years now and I'm still really happy it worked out the way it did. I love my coworkers, who have become my good friends and my job is a source of comfort and joy for me.

In the time since my divorce, I relived the college years I never really had. I engaged in drinking and partying and doing things for the pure pleasure of them. I've taken a lot of trips and enjoyed the single life with my girlfriends. I found that friendships really are crucial to healing. When I first separated, my social circle was very small. I'm grateful that I now know the importance of having many enriching relationships and not relying on one person to meet my emotional needs. Thank goodness for girlfriends!

On the relationship front, the ride has been a bumpy one. During the separation, I was in such a vulnerable and lonely state. A friend of mine introduced me to one of their friends and he and I began seeing each other. He was "recovering" from a break-up after a seven year relationship at the same time and we offered each other a lot of comfort and support. It was exciting and he helped me feel like I was ok again. My divorce left me feeling, at times, unattractive and unworthy of love. I wondered if there had been something really wrong with me that made my ex-husband leave like that. Being with this man helped me feel alive and beautiful. It awakened my sexuality and made me realize that I wasn't doomed to a life devoid of passion and love.

Early on, there were some issues that made it evident to me that this wouldn't be a lifetime love. I was honest with him and told him I didn't see a long term future. We really enjoyed each other's company and had a nice friendship with some extracurricular fun. It lasted for two years.

Around the time I got my new job and moved out of my mom's place, I finally felt like I had returned and it became clear the relationship had run its course. I wasn't able to cut it off until I was emotionally ready to invest myself fully with someone new. It was more difficult than expected, but when the time was right we parted. We've been able to remain friends.

As I was adjusting to my new single life in my new condo, I reconnected with an old high school friend who I had dated a bit back in the day. We had lost touch over the years, but I had always thought of him, and, apparently, he of me. When we saw each other there was definitely a strong chemistry between us. He was working overseas doing military contract work and was about to leave again. We exchanged contact information and kept in touch over the next several months while he was away. He returned for a family visit that Christmas and our attraction was unmistakable. He ended up staying with me for the duration of his two week visit. I was really a goner at that point. This was something real and we both knew it. Our contact was limited because he was working in another country. In retrospect, I think it's no coincidence that I chose a long distance relationship. He was also healing from a relationship in which their engagement had been broken off abruptly. We had a lot in common on the emotional front and were both hesitant, but excited about each other.

Over the next few years, there were a lot of struggles within this relationship on both sides. We each had a lot of baggage. Mine had definitely impacted our communication. I was constantly paranoid that he'd hold back and I tried very hard, if subconsciously, not to invest myself too much for fear I would be blindsided again. Naturally, this is a terrible idea if you actually want to form a stable bond. He would tell me that I created reasons to be unhappy. I couldn't just "be" myself. I was restless. I was so into him and yet, so panicked. I was so afraid of being in love again and I pushed him away over and over, even as I wanted him to prove his undying love for me. We have a deep connection and there is no one in the world that fascinates me so much and drives me so crazy. To this day, we have an extreme amount of passion and love for each other even though our relationship has ended. He taught me that passionate, consuming love is possible and, honestly, that love is what it's all about. It was a difficult relationship, but I know that's not his fault or mine that it didn't work. We have a beautiful son together and will always be bonded by parenthood.

Looking back, therapy would have been a great idea, but I wanted to "be strong." Ironically, I have my undergrad degree in Psychology and ALWAYS advise other people to seek counseling when they are having difficulties, as I believe in its benefits, but I just wouldn't accept that I could have benefited too. I see the mistake of my stubbornness and would strongly suggest it for anyone post-divorce.

I've learned a lot along the way, gained an independence I never would have discovered if I'd stayed married and I have grown as a person. I know myself better and am more comfortable in my own skin. I also have richer friendships, I love deeper, feel more and I've become a much more compassionate person.

I'm now a tenured teacher and purchased my own home. I love knowing that I can take care of myself. I'm financially stable and feel empowered that I can do this alone. I'm single right now and hope that the lessons I've learned will allow me to forge a happy and healthy relationship in the future, but right now my focus is on my son and savoring every joyful moment that motherhood has brought to me. The journey continues one day at a time. I hope that anyone reading this will keep faith that it will get better and you will be ok. Just take it one day at a time.

Michelle Denicola Poole

I'm living the dream I had several years ago, only the man in the dream is completely different. After graduating college, I remember being happily married ringing in the New Year as a newlywed who knew exactly what the future held for us – a house, PhD, baby, baby, and baby. Seventeen months later, that dream unraveled before any of those things came true for us. I found myself alone within two years of that New Year's Eve, separated and divorced.

I was determined, following the divorce, to find ways to be "me" again. I joined a local volleyball league with a new friend I had made at work. I ended up meeting my current husband looking my worst in a baggy t-shirt, cheer shorts and a ponytail sans make-up.

When I first started dating my husband, I chose to be very honest about my past. He did not accept it easily, but did reflect on the bible and through scripture began to see beyond that part of who I was. Truthfully, we hardly ever discussed the divorce. We dated for over a year before I was willing to think that the relationship could be more. On his 32nd birthday, after his birthday dinner with my family, he surprised me by asking for another "gift" – for me to be his wife. We were married in a Roman Catholic ceremony at St. Paul's Cathedral in Pittsburgh. Our ceremony was small and we had a dinner for our guests at a historical train station in the city – perfect for us.

A month after our wedding we found out we were expecting our first child. In that same month, my only living grandparent was admitted to the hospital and we watched her slowly lose her life to a variety of ailments. She would never live to see my child born. Also, during this time my Mom was admitted to the hospital repeatedly for heart related issues. My parents made the decision for her to undergo open heart surgery at 54 years of age. I faced death and scary life changing decisions during my first pregnancy. What I faced in divorce seems minute compared to what I dealt with during my pregnancy, but I had my husband, who proved to be the man I needed, walking with me, offering support and encouraging me.

Even though this time was difficult, I loved being pregnant. The awesome responsibility to grow a life within me was amazing. I never had normal symptoms of pregnancy and truly felt like I was glowing. My first born was due on 9-11 and I was excited to have such a tragic day be a day of hope for my family. Benjamin arrived four days late and full of energy. During delivery, I broke my tailbone, but this was nothing compared to what lie ahead. I was excited and overjoyed at becoming a parent, but I didn't feel connected to my son. I knew I loved him, but I didn't know what to do with him.

My Mom was still in recovery from her surgery but was able to help me daily with the tasks of motherhood. I nursed for 13 months and didn't sleep for more than three consecutive hours for the first six months. Slowly, I felt as though my world was unraveling again and those around me began to realize something was seriously wrong with me. I just wasn't acting like a normal Mom. I was uptight, anxious and unfocused. I was, in fact, facing post-partum anxiety. Luckily, my husband and I dealt with it through prayer and a strong base of friends who helped me through the day to day stuff and after six months of motherhood with a healed tailbone, I remember actually loving my son and enjoying my time with him. He and I are now bonded tightly together – I call him Momma's Boy, Mommy's Monkey and all sorts of goofy names, but for a while I was not sure I could even be his Mom.

I'm still a practicing Catholic and my husband considers himself a Christian. He attends mass with me weekly and we openly talked about scripture, homilies and church practices, but I never asked him to convert to my church. I felt that since he was a Christian that was enough for me this time around. He surprised me one summer evening by letting me know he wanted to go through RCIA (Rite of Christian Initiation of Adults) at our church. It was an honor to see him become an active part of my faith practices. He wanted to be sure we were raising our family together in a faith based not only on Christianity, but on Catholic practices. In my current marriage, we work together daily on our faith and relationship which is something I dearly cherish.

While we were newlyweds and expectant parents, we started looking for a home – two and half years of looking proved fruitless. We wanted specific details in a house and knew we were not home improvers so we left ourselves with few options. We decided to build a house only to find out we were expecting again.

During my second pregnancy, we built our house; a house which met all of our needs, specifications, and desires. My second son, Anthony, was born surprisingly three weeks early; catching everyone off-guard. We had nothing ready and were looking forward to spending those final weeks of pregnancy making final decisions on the house - brick, windows, siding, kitchen, lighting, and the like. My husband tackled all the house needs, while encouraging another post-partum anxious, sleep-deprived Mom. This time my anxiety was not about the baby, but rather about not being able to love and attend to my 27 month old, diaper-wearing, newly-speaking toddler.

With so much going on, I sought help from my doctor and was put on a low dose of anti-anxiety medication. They helped me deal with the little things that would work me up and allowed me to actually sleep when appropriate - something I struggled to do after my first child was born.

The house got built, we moved, but our townhouse, which we were selling in order to recover our savings, never sold due to the real estate market. We found ourselves in a financial position we didn't plan for. I needed to return to work months sooner than intended (although I must admit I was blessed with a year maternity leave the first time around and nearly ten months the second). Returning to work as a Mom of two was challenging, but I met it with the support of my husband again who helps me 100% with household activities and children responsibilities.

My husband is a man of faith, stability and discipline which compliments my energy, enthusiasm and anxiety. He walks with me through the turmoil and proves to me, daily, how the little things matter the most. We can face the challenges that lie ahead knowing that we have endured hardships and blessings together.

I'm a woman of strength and perseverance; I believe this now. I try to deal with hardships remembering that someday I will laugh again and I hope that I will learn from it. This is what the last few years have taught me. Life does exist, improve, change and still hurt after divorce. After all, it is life. But divorce doesn't define my life; rather, it's become a thing that happened in my distant past.

Michelle Joyce

Looking back to my wedding day, I don't recognize the girl I was then. During my first marriage, I was unsure of whom I was and because of that I married the wrong man. After eight years together, I emerged from the divorce literally not knowing who I was and what I wanted.

Since then, I feel as if I've been reborn. I spent a lot of time, post-divorce, remembering what made me "me." I focused on what I wanted out of life. It was the first time I had done that. What I discovered was surprising. When I was married I could have written a list five pages long of all the things I needed to change about myself. I felt like if I changed who I was, I would make my husband happy. What I discovered after the divorce was that I was okay just the way I am. It wasn't me that had the problem; it was the combination of him plus me. We were wrong together.

Very soon after my separation, I met a wonderful man. It was the classic case of great guy, wrong timing. I was not ready to be in a relationship. I spent so much time, during my marriage, focusing my attention on someone else's needs that I wanted to spend some time focusing on myself. So I did. We started to see each other, but he respected that I needed time and space. He gave it to me and never questioned why.

When I was ready for more, he was there. We married and had our first daughter that year. When our daughter turned one, I decided to take a dance class to get into shape and to meet other people. Being a stay-at-home mom, though rewarding, can be isolating. I went to a local dance studio to take an adult class. It was there that I rediscovered my love of dance; a passion that I thought faded many years ago. My husband supported me 100%. One class became two classes and, before I knew it, I was offered a job teaching.

Through my work at the dance studio and through a local MOM's Club, I have met wonderful women who have become great friends. Unlike my first husband, who hated my friends, my husband supports my relationships knowing that it helps me be a better wife and mother. Four years after the birth of our first daughter, we welcomed our second daughter. And we also gave birth to our dream home where we plan to grow old together.

There are some days where I sit staring at my family and I'm amazed at the life I've created for myself. After the divorce, I couldn't fathom being happy again. It seemed like I would never be a mother, never meet another man and never find passion in my life. Now, I feel so blessed at what God has given me.

At our wedding, my husband and I danced our first dance to "God Bless the Broken Road." It was the perfect song for us. I had a broken road because of divorce, but that road led me to where I was supposed to be and to be the person I was meant to become.

You're One of Us.
Embrace Being Fabulous!

The four of us are very dear friends. We met during such sad, depressing times in our lives when our marriages were disintegrating and our futures seemed bleak. The bond that formed during that time has made us sisters, *divorce sisters*. We've been by each other's sides ever since. We've been there to support each other, mourn the losses, and cheer for the successes and, most importantly, to remind one another how far we've come. We've never been able to get all of us together, but we keep up with each other through the internet and through phone calls. Our sisterhood has been the foundation that helped us rebuild our lives and helped us become young, divorced and fabulous! We hope that by sharing our journeys and friendship with you, that you also feel a part of this sisterhood and that you feel inspired to embrace your second chance.

You're one of us now. Make us proud. Go out there and be fabulous!

Vows for a Young, Divorced and Fabulous New Life

As you embrace your second chance, carefully choose the vows that will inspire you along your new path. Think about what is important to you and how you want to feel. Below are the promises that we've chosen to make. Use them as a guide for what you want to create in your life. Take the time to commit yourself to living the best life possible.

1. *I promise* to be completely honest with myself, to acknowledge what I feel and to release those feelings so it can be transformed into something positive in my life.

2. *I promise* to listen to my intuition and trust its guidance.

3. *I promise* to commit myself wholly to the things I hold sacred.

4. *I promise* to allow myself to be the woman that my soul yearns to be and to follow the passions that dwell inside of me.

5. *I promise* to love and cherish myself each and every day, with complete acceptance.

6. *I promise* to have fun, embrace joy and feel fabulous!

Made in the USA
Lexington, KY
13 May 2016